Telling Time

In association with Esso UK plc

Telling Time

Alexander Sturgis

National Gallery Company, London
Distributed by Yale University Press

Supported by Esso

This book was published to accompany an exhibition at
The National Gallery, London
18 October 2000 – 14 January 2001

First published in Great Britain in 2000 by
National Gallery Company Limited
St Vincent House, 30 Orange Street, London WC2H 7HH
www.nationalgallery.co.uk

ISBN 1 85709 905 2
525467

British Library Cataloguing-in-Publication Data
A catalogue record is available from the British Library

Designer Tim Harvey
Editor Tom Windross
Picture Researcher Xenia Geroulanos

Printed and bound in Great Britain by Butler and Tanner,
Frome and London

Jacket illustration: *Saint John the Baptist retiring to the Desert*
(detail), Giovanni di Paolo, cat. no. 6
Title page illustration: 'Dancing Couple' from *Animal Locomotion*
(detail), Eadweard Muybridge, cat. no. 22

Author's acknowledgements

I would like to thank my many colleagues at the National
Gallery, National Gallery Company and the lending institutions
who have helped in the preparation of this book and the
exhibition it accompanies. Special thanks are also due to: Anna
Benn, Judy Egerton, John Findlay, Antony Griffiths, Mark
Haworth-Booth, Stephen Herbert, Charles Heywood, Michael
Kauffman, Robert Kentridge, Alastair Laing, Kristin Lippincott,
James Lomax, John Lowden, Sir Denis Mahon, Anthony Wells-
Cole and Catherine Whistler.

The eye-tracking experiment described in the chapter Time to
Look has been mounted in collaboration with the Applied Vision
Reseach Unit, Institute of Behavioural Sciences, University of
Derby. I would particularly like to thank Lyndsey Cobb, Alastair
Gale, Mark Mugglestone, Kevin Purdy and David Wooding.

As the experiment develops, results will be posted on a special
website: http://ibs.derby.ac.uk/gallery

CONTENTS

SPONSOR'S FOREWORD

IT IS OUR PLEASURE to continue our long association with the National Gallery through this fascinating *Telling Time* exhibition that focuses on the relationship between time and painting.

We hope you enjoy exploring the theme through the paintings and will also take the opportunity to participate in the largest ever eye-tracking experiment that examines the process of looking at images. The special audio tour that takes in seventeen paintings in the permanent collection provides yet another chance to improve our understanding of the many wonderful masterpieces held at the Gallery.

It is particularly appropriate for us to be sponsoring an exhibition called *Telling Time*. Since we first sponsored an exhibition here in 1988, the passage of time has seen significant changes in our organisation. Now, as we progress into the new millennium, Esso UK looks forward to a challenging future as a member of the newly-formed worldwide ExxonMobil Group.

The passage of time affects us all. The year 2000 is a momentous time in our lives and The Millennium Esso Exhibition at the National Gallery affords the ideal opportunity to look at how artists have depicted it in their images.

Once again, we are delighted to be able to play our part in supporting the Gallery in its very worthwhile objective of increasing public understanding and appreciation of its vast array of treasures.

Ansel Condray
Chairman, Esso UK plc

DIRECTOR'S FOREWORD

THIS LITTLE BOOK surveys a huge range of images, from comic strips to some of the greatest art produced in western Europe. It tackles in small compass two very big questions – time in pictures and pictures in time – setting out to look at how artists have tried to paint the results of time passing, as objects move or stories progress; how long we, as visitors and viewers, take to scan and then to read a picture; and how over the centuries time modifies or destroys what the painter originally wanted us to see.

Like all big questions they are unlikely to yield precise answers, but are, for that very reason, profoundly worth asking. We have become so used to the idea of a picture not just showing a situation but telling a story, that we have forgotten what an extraordinary idea this is. To understand even a little better how artists engage us in narrative and how the eye decodes an image as complex and conventionalised as a European painting, is to be roused to an even more intense pleasure and admiration. And deepening the pleasure given by pictures is the main purpose of the National Gallery.

Our heaviest responsibility, however, is, without doubt, to protect the pictures from the effects of time, so that many years from now they may still be enjoyed as nearly as possible as the artists intended. Both the Conservation and Scientific Departments of the Gallery are dedicated to this task and over the last fifty years, they have led the world in deepening our understanding of how pictures were made and how they have changed.

Paintings may be subject to time, but since classical antiquity, it has been a commonplace of poetry that only two things on earth can withstand the destroying years: art and friendship. Without the loyal friendship of Esso, the National Gallery's most generous and longest-standing sponsor, we could not have presented this exhibition nor the eleven Esso Exhibitions that have preceded it. All of us who work in the National Gallery would like to express to them our heartfelt thanks.

Neil MacGregor
Director

About Time

Harmen Steenwyck's *Still Life* (fig. 1), painted in the Netherlands in about 1640, is clearly a painting about time. A chronometer sits open on the table measuring out time's passage and beside it is a skull as a symbol of time's end. It is a picture intended to remind us of life's brevity – no more substantial than the thin trail of smoke from the snuffed-out lamp. But it is also supposed to prepare us for eternity; reminding us of the lasting truths of religion by measuring them against the fleeting pleasures of earthly wealth, learning and the senses – symbolised by the precious objects, books and musical instruments. It is one of countless paintings produced in Europe, from the Renaissance onwards, intended to perform the very same task.

Fig. 1 Harmen Steenwyck, *Still Life: An Allegory of the Vanities of Human Life*, c.1640, oil on oak, 39.2 × 50.7 cm, London, National Gallery

Skulls, snuffed-out candles, bubbles, overturned glasses and all kinds of timepieces proliferate in so-called *vanitas* imagery – perhaps the most familiar and obvious way in which painters have given the subject of passing time visual expression. The term *vanitas* comes from the Old Testament (Ecclesiastes 1:2 'vanity of vanities … all is vanity') in a passage that appeals for the rejection of the concerns of this world – wealth, sensual pleasure, power – in preparation for the next. *Vanitas* themes proliferated in the seventeenth century, particularly in the

Netherlands and Spain where they were repeated to the point of banality in a wide range of different paintings. These included *vanitas* still lifes produced in huge quantities; portraits, in which skulls and other *memento mori* (reminders of death) were familiar props from the sixteenth century; and devotional paintings of saints, particularly Jerome and Mary Magdalene who were often shown, skull in hand, meditating on past sins and future judgement. Innumerable genre scenes carried the same sombre message. To a seventeenth-century viewer Caspar Netscher's *Two Boys blowing Bubbles* (fig. 2) would have been legible immediately as an allegory of life's fragility. These paintings have time as their subject: they embody a linear view of time which flows from a beginning to an all too imminent end – an end that is both personal and cosmic.

The props of *vanitas* paintings were not the only elements of the iconography of time. Serial images showing the progress of human life from infancy to old age, or the pointed juxtaposition of a child with an old man or woman, could carry similar messages about life's inexorable progress and death's inevitability. In a separate tradition, and one which embodies the contrasting notion of time as cyclical rather than linear, artists from the Middle Ages onwards were accustomed to depicting cycles showing the characteristic labours of the months or seasons (figs. 3 and 4).

Fig. 2 Caspar Netscher, *Two Boys blowing Bubbles*, c.1670, oil on oak, 31.2 × 24.6 cm, London, National Gallery

Fig. 3 David Teniers the Younger, *Spring*, *c*.1664, oil on copper, 22.1 × 16.5 cm, London, National Gallery

Fig. 4 David Teniers the Younger, *Winter*, *c*.1664, oil on copper, 22.2 × 16.2 cm, London, National Gallery

Time could also appear in person. In Batoni's allegory *Time orders Old Age to destroy Beauty* (fig. 5), the subject is once again the ravages of age but Time is now personified, taking an active role in the disfigurement of the fresh-faced figure of 'Beauty'. Batoni, working in Rome in the eighteenth century, was particularly proud of this painting, boasting to his patron that the subject was entirely of his 'own invention'. However original the conception, the figure of Time follows well-established lines. He is old, winged (because time flies) and carries a hourglass – one of his common attributes, the other being the scythe. This familiar figure of 'Father Time' is not as old as he seems: although he often appears in allegorical paintings as a companion of the gods of Greece or Rome and elements of his iconography can be traced back to the ancient world, he is actually a late medieval invention.[1] His character is also contrary: he can be destructive, as in Batoni's allegory or when shown clipping the

wings of Love or wielding his scythe, but he can also be benign – protecting, or more often revealing, his daughter Truth in all her naked beauty.

The iconography of time is an immensely rich and varied subject, but it becomes richer still when considered in the context of painting – both as an object and as an act – and its relation to the passage of time. In Holbein's portrait of *Jean de Dinteville and Georges de Selve*, known as *The Ambassadors* (fig. 6), many elements familiar from later *vanitas* imagery are present. The famously distorted skull stretched out between the sitters is an explicit (if hidden) reminder of death. The higher of the two shelves between them is laden with instruments – such as sundials and quadrants – nearly all of which were used to tell the time. There have been many interpretations of the painting and the objects within it, but clearly one intended emphasis was on the brevity of life and the futility of worldly wealth and accomplishments. But while the painting may

Fig. 5 Pompeo Batoni, *Time orders Old Age to destroy Beauty*, 1746, oil on canvas, 135.3 × 96.5 cm, London, National Gallery

carry such a message, it also contradicts it. Jean de Dinteville, on the left, may well have been accustomed to meditate upon his own mortality (he wears a skull badge on his cap to reinforce the point), but he also had himself painted with an eye to posterity. Every portrait is commemorative. For Dürer, writing a generation earlier, portraiture performed one of the principal roles of art, which was to 'preserve the likenesses of men after their deaths'. In this sense, at least, painting could cheat time. In common with many portraits, the ages of Holbein's sitters are carefully noted ('29' on de Dinteville's dagger and '25' on the book under de Selve's elbow). This, the painting claims, is how its sitters appeared at this particular time: Holbein included the date, 1533, beneath his signature and it has been claimed that the shadows cast on the polyhedral sundial to the left of de Selve's elbow record the hour (fig. 7). Common sense might reject such a notion (there is no direct sunlight and the sundial's design is problematic as it appears to have been adapted to tell the time in North African latitudes), but there are portraits dated to the day and, on rare occasions, to the hour.[2] Any claim to such exactitude raises more questions: *The*

Fig. 6 Hans Holbein the Younger, *The Ambassadors*, 1533, oil on oak, 207 × 209.5 cm, London, National Gallery

Fig. 7 Hans Holbein the Younger, *The Ambassadors* (detail), 1533, oil on oak, 207 × 209.5 cm, London, National Gallery

Fig. 8 Paolo Veronese, *The Vision of Saint Helena*, c.1560–5, oil on canvas, 197.5 × 115.6 cm, London, National Gallery

Fig. 9 Paolo Veronese, digital impression of *The Vision of Saint Helena* with restored blue background

Ambassadors is a painting that self-evidently took time to paint. It may mark the visit in the summer of 1533 of Georges de Selve, bishop of Lavaur, to his friend de Dinteville, then resident in London, but we can be confident that the picture was unfinished when the churchman left the country. It is, of course, the extravagant detail that encourages us to search for meaning in its every brushstroke. It is even tempting (granted the absence of any sun) to see the shadows of the sundial as reflecting the passage of time during the painting's making, for although one of the faces clearly shows the time as 9.30, on the two others an hour has elapsed and it is 10.30.

The idea that art could preserve and prolong the fame and glory – quite apart from the physical appearance – of its subject or painter was encapsulated in the motto, popular from the sixteenth century, *vita brevis ars longa* (life is short, art is long). But of course art isn't as long as all that. Paintings too are subject to time, they crack and flake, colours change, fade or darken. Usually we know when we are looking at a badly damaged picture, but some effects of time are less obvious. Veronese's poetic image of the dreaming Saint Helena is not obviously ravaged by time, but the painting has changed irredeemably. The sky was painted with smalt, a notoriously fugitive pigment, and what now appears as overcast was once an intense blue, which can be re-created on a computer screen but not on the canvas (figs. 8 and 9).

Paintings may outlive us, but any attempt to survive through art is, in the end, as futile as any of the other bulwarks put up against the inexorable flow of time. *Vanitas* images sometimes include paintings or prints – at times visibly disintegrating – as *vanitas* objects themselves.[3] Using paintings within paintings in this way also draws attention to the rich and fruitful tension in all *vanitas* imagery between the message and the medium. Although Steenwyck's *Still Life* may preach against the world of the senses and worldly wealth, it is designed to appeal to those senses and is itself a precious object. What is more, it too – like the curling pages of the book propped on the skull – will suffer from the effects of time. As it happens, the painting has suffered already in a particularly striking and suggestive way. In the body of the stone bottle there is, just visible, the shadowy profile of a man (fig. 10). This shows Steenwyck's

original intention was to include a stone bust – probably of a Roman emperor as a symbol of earthly power – where the jug now stands. Changing his mind he painted it out, but oil paint's tendency to become more translucent with age has resulted in its ghostly presence. In this particular image it seems a remarkably fitting demonstration of the fragility and transience of paint itself.

Paintings such as Holbein's *Ambassadors* and Steenwyck's *Still Life* suggest some of the various ways in which paintings have both taken time as a subject and are themselves subject to time. But paintings relate to time in other ways. The last part of this book considers the act of looking at pictures as a process that takes place over time, but it is another aspect of time's relation to painting that is the focus of this book and the exhibition it accompanies: here we are concerned not with how painters have approached time as a subject, but how they have struggled with the apparent limitations of their medium to depict the passage of time itself.

Fig. 10 Harmen Steenwyck, *Still Life: An Allegory of the Vanities of Human Life* (detail), *c*.1640, oil on oak, 39.2 × 50.7 cm. London, National Gallery

Story Time

STORIES as written in books, or told in speech, take time. At their simplest they progress from a 'once upon a time' to a 'happily ever after', but even those stories whose telling is circuitous, which flash back and jump forward, unfold over time in a way and at a pace controlled by the teller. Pictures on the other hand are, in one sense at least, timeless. To employ a distinction much used in the eighteenth century, painting is an 'art of space' in contrast to poetry or music, the 'arts of time'. But if you cannot talk meaningfully of a painting's beginning, middle or end, how can a still and silent picture 'tell a story' that develops over time?

One possible response to this question is to deny that pictures can *tell* stories at all. Most narrative paintings illustrate known stories and rely on the viewer recognising the story to be understood: someone who knew nothing of the Bible would be more likely to interpret a painting of Adam and Eve as a scene of naturist apple-eaters than to reconstruct the story of the 'Fall of Man' from the book of Genesis. One of the most famous and repeated pronouncements on the use of paintings, made by Pope Gregory the Great around 600, suggested that pictures should be displayed in churches so that the illiterate 'may at least read by seeing on the walls what they are unable to read in books', but paintings in churches can never have communicated their meaning independently. They might remind the illiterate viewer of stories they had heard, or they could make the stories more vivid and encourage their contemplation, but they could not tell them from scratch. This might seem a limitation, but it is precisely because this is the way that most narrative paintings work – reminding the viewer of a familiar story rather than telling a new tale – that time can indeed pass within them. Although we may recognise separate episodes or see evidence of past actions or intimations of future events in a painting, even where we do not, we naturally project forward and back to make the image stand for the whole story. By this argument, it is the viewer who puts time into paintings.

THE COMIC STRIP AND PICTURE CYCLES

There is, however, a familiar way in which images can have beginnings and ends and can consequently 'tell', rather than merely illustrate, a story: the comic strip (cat. no. 1, overleaf). By presenting a sequence of images to be 'read' from frame to frame, the progression of the story over time is re-established. We read comic books from left to right and top to bottom as we would read a page of writing. Of course, most comic strips combine their images with words, and where they do so it is once again the words that control the pace and order of narration: single frames can contain speeches or whole conversations that might imply a time span of several minutes. However, although most comic strips rely on words to be understood, text is not always essential. The wordless comic strip can also be legible – even if understanding may depend on a familiarity with the conventions of the genre and, more importantly, the story is limited to dealing with the general and archetypal rather than the particular and specific. We seldom know what anyone is called in a wordless strip, even if we are expected to recognise their essential characteristics.

Although we might think of the comic book as a relatively recent form, there is absolutely nothing new about using a sequence of images to tell a story. One of the earliest surviving pieces of narrative art, the so-called *Royal Standard of Ur* (now in the British Museum) of 2600 BC, tells in six scenes the still-legible

Cat. no. 1 Hergé (Georges Rémi, 1907–83), from *The Adventures of Tintin: Prisoners of the Sun*
First published 1949, English edition, 1962
© Hergé Moulinsart 2000. English Translation Egmont Children's Books

story of a victorious battle followed by a triumphal feast.[1] Compared with this ancient prototype the earliest surviving illuminated books appear positively recent, but in these too we can find the familiar division of pages into sequences of separate, framed images. One of the earliest surviving biblical manuscripts, the sixth-century Italian *Saint Augustine Gospels*, contains a full-page illumination in which twelve small scenes show the events leading up to the crucifixion. This manuscript was in Canterbury from at least the eighth century and, according to tradition, had been taken there by Saint Augustine himself on his mission to covert the English in 597. It was almost certainly this venerable precedent that inspired the creation, in twelfth-century Canterbury, of one of the most extensive narrative sequences of New Testament scenes ever produced.

This sequence is to be found on four sheets that are now divided between New York and London, but were once attached to a manuscript known as *The Eadwine Psalter* (cat. no. 2).[2] The side of the sheet shown covers the story of Christ's Passion, from his trial before Annas and Caiaphas the High Priests at the top left, to the descent from the cross at bottom right. At first perusal it appears that scene follows scene in a straightforward temporal progression, but in fact the artists exploited the rich possibilities offered by the comic strip format in depicting the unfolding of a narrative over time. The sheet is divided into twelve separate squares. A number of these are further subdivided and in most of these cases one simply reads the scene in the top half as preceding the one below it: in the third square down on the left, Christ carries his cross before being relieved of his burden by Simon of Cyrene. In the top row of the sheet, however, something rather more ingenious is going on. The first two squares are subdivided but the top and bottom halves are telling

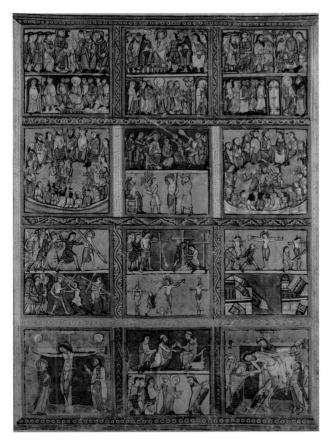

Cat. no. 2 English, Leaf from *The Eadwine Psalter*
Mid-twelfth century, watercolour on paper, 39.5 × 29.2 cm
London, The Victoria and Albert Museum

two separate stories that we are meant to read as happening simultaneously – as we would read a split screen in the cinema. Above, Christ is first brought before the high priests and is then beaten by one of his officers. Below we see Saint Peter who during this time denied Christ three times. In depicting these two parallel stories the artist has relied on two separate Gospels: the trials of Christ as told in the Gospel of John (John 18:13–24) and the denials of Saint Peter, told in Luke (Luke 22:55–62).[3] Of course we can only recognise this with reference to the Gospel accounts. It is because this is a familiar story that the artists can play such sophisticated temporal games: without knowledge of the text the relationship of the scenes would be as unclear as the actions they contained.

Narrative cycles of this kind were found not only in manuscripts but also painted on the walls and windows of medieval churches – although not always intended to be read from left to right or top to bottom.[4] In domestic interiors, biblical and mythological narrative cycles were painted on furniture or set into panelling, a popular form of interior decoration in Renaissance Italy. None of these cycles survives in its original setting and many panels have been cut from the furniture on which they were painted, such as the two delightful scenes by a Florentine artist known as The Master of the Judgement of Paris, which may once have been part of a *cassone* or chest (cat. no. 3, overleaf).[5] The two scenes are from the story of Apollo and Daphne, as related in Ovid's *Metamorphoses*. In the first the god Apollo, shot by one of Cupid's arrows, is pursuing the less-than-eager Daphne. In the next he is about to catch her, but in that instant – and in answer to her prayers – she escapes his clutches and the worst of his intentions by turning into a laurel tree. Strangely, Apollo changes clothes between one frame and the next, but the scenes are also unusual in showing two moments following each other in such swift succession, like two successive frames from a film.

These panels may have formed part of a larger cycle, but the whole story could not have been told in such detail. Pictorial cycles vary the pace of their narration, concentrating on those 'telling' moments by which we recognise the tale. In this case the apparent split-second gap between the two scenes was also the result of a particular pictorial problem – how do you show someone turning instantaneously from woman to tree?

The painter of these scenes, like the illuminators of *The Eadwine Psalter*, could rely on his audience knowing and recognising the story he depicted. However, in the eighteenth century the English artist William Hogarth turned his attention to painting series of pictures that told stories of his own devising. Hogarth claimed that in producing what he called his 'modern moral subjects' he was entering 'a Field unbroke up in any Country or any age', but he was perhaps flattering himself. There already existed a tradition of popular printed broadsheets that combined text and images to tell popular, contemporary and often moral tales which Hogarth was adapting.[6] His enterprise was new in the realm of high art, however, and in the wit and sophistication of his narratives. Hogarth's tales are told in sequences of

Cat. no. 3 Master of the Judgement of Paris, *Daphne pursued by Apollo*
Mid-fifteenth century, oil on wood, 47.5 × 53.1 cm
Birmingham, The Barber Institute of Fine Arts, The University of Birmingham

Cat. no. 3 Master of the Judgement of Paris, *The Metamorphosis of Daphne*
Mid-fifteenth century, oil on wood, 47.5 × 53.1 cm
Birmingham, The Barber Institute of Fine Arts, The University of Birmingham

Fig. 11 William Hogarth, *Rake's Progress* (first scene), 1735, engraving, 32.1 × 38.7 cm, London, The British Museum

Fig. 12 William Hogarth, *Rake's Progress* (last scene), 1735, engraving, 31.6 × 38.7 cm, London, The British Museum

images 'design'd in series and having something of that kind of connection which the pages of a book have', but they were not 'wordless'. His series of engravings were accompanied by lengthy captions to explain the tales, and even the paintings made ingenious use of cleverly contrived inscriptions on letters, newspapers and the like to identify his characters and their predicaments. In the first two 'modern moral subjects' – *A Harlot's Progress* and *A Rake's Progress* – we follow the central characters from scene to scene, witnessing them in a sequence of situations that defines the tale. It is no accident that Hogarth called each of his stories a 'progress': it is our understanding of the scenes as showing stages in a progression over time that allows us to read the Rake's inexorable decline from a young dandy having his suit fitted (fig. 11) to a half-naked man in a lunatic asylum (fig. 12). It is actually the time we understand as having passed *between* each scene that makes sense of the story. If we assumed that the eight prints of *A Rake's Progress* showed eight typical days in the life of a man about town, the sense of the narrative would, of course, collapse.

Hogarth exploited the notion of the time between his painted scenes to full and titillating effect in his pair of paintings, *Before* and *After*, which tell an altogether simpler tale (modern but not altogether moral) that needed no explanatory caption (cat. no. 4, overleaf).[7] They were painted between 1730–1, exactly the time

that Hogarth was developing the first of his 'progresses', and can claim to be the first original narrative sequence he composed and completed. The scenes, set against identical leafy backgrounds, show two moments separated by a short amount of time but an enormous amount of activity. In the first an elegant young man attempts to seduce an apparently reluctant woman. In the second they are clinging to each other in red-faced disarray and, with an explicitness unusual for Hogarth, the young man's trousers gape to reveal a penis as flushed as his features. The story is hardly sophisticated but it is crystal clear, even if the central, defining event is missing. Few are going to ask, ' "Before" and "After" what?'

The Hogarthian tradition of the 'modern moral subject' was taken up by the Victorians, who addressed society's ills with all the moral outrage, but little of the wit, of their eighteenth-century predecessor. One of the most intriguing picture series, particularly in its relation to passing time, is that of three paintings by Augustus Egg known as *Past and Present* (cat. no. 5, overleaf).[8] The title is entirely apt, but it is not Egg's own and the series may even have acquired it by mistake – it was the title of another painting, also exhibited at the Royal Academy in 1858, and seems to have become attached to Egg's paintings through a misreading of one of the exhibition reviews.[9] Egg's pictures were

Cat. no. 4 William Hogarth (1697–1764), *Before*
About 1731, oil on cavas, 37.2 × 44.7 cm
Cambridge, The Fitzwilliam Museum

Cat. no. 4 William Hogarth (1697–1764), *After*
About 1731, oil on canvas, 37.2 × 45.1 cm
Cambridge, The Fitzwilliam Museum

exhibited without a title but with a lengthy quotation in the catalogue:

> August the 4th. Have just heard that B— has been dead more than a fortnight, so his poor children have now lost both parents. I hear *she* was seen on Friday last near the Strand, evidently without a place to lay her head. What a fall hers has been.

Apart from allowing us to decipher the awful tale depicted in Egg's paintings, the passage also reflects their preoccupation with the passage of time. It is 4 August – a Wednesday in 1858 – a man named B— has been dead more than a fortnight and his wife was seen last Friday destitute and homeless near the Strand, itself a few steps away from the Royal Academy, then housed in Trafalgar Square. The passage could be the opening of a Victorian novel and of course the device of the narrator looking back from present circumstances to past events is frequently used in literature. Egg's three paintings follow the same trajectory; they are not a straightforward progress in the manner of Hogarth, but show two contrasting moments in the present (or at least 'last Friday') on either side of a defining past event. It is no surprise that Egg was a friend of Charles Dickens and Wilkie Collins, holidaying with both and acting with Dickens in amateur theatricals.

In his review of the Academy exhibition John Ruskin cleared up evident confusion as to the pictures' subject:

> In the central piece the husband discovers his wife's infidelity: he dies five years afterwards. The two lateral pictures represent the same moment of night a fortnight after his death. The same little cloud is under the moon. The two children see it from the chamber in which they are praying for their lost mother; and their mother, from behind a boat under a vault on the river shore.[10]

As Ruskin notes, Egg uses the moon and its neighbouring cloud to ensure that the scenes of the daughters and mother with her sickly bastard child are understood as being exactly the same moment in time, a device which emphasises the characters' insurmountable separation. The moment that led to their present circumstance is depicted in the dramatic central scene, whose import is reinforced

Cat. no. 5 Augustus Egg (1816–1863), *Past and Present* (Triptych) 1858, oil on canvas, each 64 × 76 cm
London, Tate

by a host of incidental and symbolic detail: the father holds the discovered love letter in his hand; a miniature of his wife's lover is crushed underfoot; the bracelets around the mother's wrists take on the appearance of handcuffs; while the cause of her fall is suggested by the French (and by implication immoral) novel by Balzac, on which the children have been building their now-toppling house of cards. Next to the woman lies an apple 'rotten to the core', on the wall is a painting of Adam and Eve being expelled from Paradise, while in the mirror we see the open door through which the mother herself will soon be expelled.

The grim subject matter of Egg's pictures caused outrage: 'There must be a line drawn as to where the horrors that should not be painted for public and innocent sight begin, and we think Mr. Egg has put one foot at least beyond this line.'[11] But there was, perhaps surprisingly, no comment on the ingenuity of his storytelling, his unique use of simultaneity and flashback.

CONTINUOUS NARRATIVE

The telling or illustration of a story in a series of separate images relies upon an understanding of their relation to passing time. Once the convention that one picture 'follows' another is accepted, sequential narrative becomes relatively straightforward. However, artists who attempt to tell a story in a single painting are faced with different problems and have resorted to different conventions. In Giovanni di Paolo's panel of *Saint John the Baptist retiring to the Desert* (cat. no. 6), the figure of the saint appears both at the gateway to the city and on the stony path leading up into the dark, jaw-like crevice of the mountain.[12] This method of combining more than one moment from a story into a single space, so that individual figures are repeated, is usually called 'continuous narrative'.[13] In many ways there is not a huge difference between continuous narrative and the picture cycle. Indeed they are often used in tandem: in *The Eadwine Psalter* leaf (cat. no. 2), Saint Peter appears twice in the second square of the top row (both before and after the cock crows), and conversely Giovanni's panel is one of a series

showing scenes from the life of Saint John. Despite the obvious similarities between the two methods, for many people continuous narrative appears both naive and illogical. It does so because of our attitudes to time and space.

Little about Giovanni's scene can be considered realistic: the figures of Saint John are far too large for the setting and the mountains into which he walks are deeply stylised, and yet it is the double appearance of the saint that can be most puzzling to a modern viewer. The artist's intention in showing the same figure more than once was clearly to indicate the passing of time: given that someone cannot be in two places at once, time must have passed between Saint John appearing at the city gate and halfway up the mountain. But viewers today often reach a different conclusion: for them Giovanni di Paolo has made the 'error' of showing Saint John in two places at the same time.

Our natural assumption when looking at a depiction of a single space seems to be that almost by definition it must show a single moment in time. It is tempting to blame this assumption on the primacy of the photograph in today's visual culture, but in fact the idea that a picture should depict only a single moment long predates photography. It was, for example, a commonplace of eighteenth-century criticism. The painter and President of the Royal Academy James Barry was one of many who criticised those 'defective … old painters who employed different points of time in the same view' overlooking the fact that those defectives included artists he championed elsewhere, such as Michelangelo and Raphael.[14]

It has often been argued that the death knell of 'continuous narrative' was sounded by the invention of one point linear perspective. A perspective picture presupposes a spectator who is stationary, their eye fixed opposite the picture's single vanishing point. In one of the most famous early accounts of perspective, the fifteenth-century Italian Alberti likened a painting to an open window through which we look into a single imaginary space. By this argument, to have more than a single moment in time shown in such a view runs counter to the painting's realism.

Cat. no. 6 Giovanni di Paolo (active by 1417; died 1482), *Saint John the Baptist retiring to the Desert*
Probably about 1453, tempera on wood, 31.1 × 38.8 cm
London, National Gallery

Although this account has a certain internal logic, it falls apart when examined in light of the surviving paintings. Continuous narrative actually thrived in the fifteenth and sixteenth centuries. In fact it seems to have been used more in the fifteenth century than in the fourteenth, even by many of the artists usually credited with making the most significant advances in the realistic depiction of space, such as Ghiberti and Massaccio.[15] In a fascinating passage written in the early 1490s, Leonardo da Vinci's insistence on spatial logic actually leads him to recommend continuous narrative. Writing about the decoration of chapel walls Leonardo attacked as the 'height of stupidity' the common practice of placing multiple scenes, each with its own separate vanishing point, in tiers on the wall – resulting in the absurdity of buildings in one scene appearing above the sky of the scene below, and so on:

> If you ask me: how shall I paint on one wall the life of a saint which is divided into many incidents? My answer is that you must place the first plane at the eye level of the beholder of the scene and on that plane represent the first scene in a large size, and then diminishing the figures and the buildings on the various hills and plains, as you go on, make the setting for the whole story. And as to the remainder of the wall, fill it with large trees in relation to the figures, or with angels, if they fit the story, or perhaps birds or clouds. If you do otherwise you will exert yourself in vain and all your work will go awry.[16]

For Leonardo a single believable space certainly does not imply a single moment in time. On the contrary,

Fig. 13 Nicolò dell'Abate, *The Death of Eurydice*, c.1552–71, oil on canvas, 189.2 × 237.5 cm, London, National Gallery

Fig. 14 Joachim Wtewael, *The Marriage of Peleus and Thetis*, 1612, oil on copper, 36.5 × 42 cm, Williamstown, Sterling and Francine Clark Institute

in time became increasingly prevalent, painters did not abandon the continuous method completely. The Utrecht artist Joachim Wtewael followed well-established convention when, in *The Judgement of Paris* (cat. no. 7), he included the preceding scene of the wedding feast of Peleus and Thetis in the woods behind.[17] It was at this wedding that Eris, the goddess of discord, provoked the quarrel between Venus, Juno and Minerva as to who was the fairest, which led to the recruitment of the shepherd Paris as an impartial judge. In this instance we look back in time and space – the smaller scene providing the background to both story and painting – but despite the fittingness of this arrangement it was not universal. Leonardo recommended that the 'first' scene be placed in the foreground, by which he probably meant the 'most important' (the Italian word he used, *primo*, can mean both), but the most important scene can either precede or come after subsidiary episodes in a story. Indeed, which moment an artist chooses for the 'principal' scene will vary according to his or her intentions. Wtewael produced a number of paintings of the wedding feast of Peleus and Thetis (fig. 14), and in these it is the judgement of Paris that we find being conducted by ghostly figures in the distance – a glimpse of the future rather than a look back to the past.

The ghostly aspect and silvery hue that Wtewael gives to the figures at the wedding feast in his painting *The Judgement of Paris* may simply be a means of suggesting their distance in space – the effect of atmospheric perspective – but it is possible that their spectral appearance was also intended to imply their presence in the past: to suggest we are looking at them through the mists of time. In his *Marriage of Peleus and Thetis* the small figures of Paris and the three goddesses are noticeably more ethereal than those in the kitchen next to them. This practice was recommended by the writer Franciscus Junius in his work *The Painting of the Ancients* first published in 1637, just before Wtewael's death, which laid out a theory of painting based on the selective quotation of ancient writers. Junius clearly had no theoretical objection to more than a single moment being represented in a painting, indeed, like Leonardo, he recommends it.

the construction of realistic space in depth increased the opportunities for the ingenious disposition of the different episodes one wished to include.

Continuous narrative survived throughout the sixteenth century and beyond. As one example of many, Niccolò dell'Abate's *Death of Eurydice* (fig. 13) painted in the 1550s or 60s shows the nymph twice, once fleeing the eager grasp of Aristaeus and then dead on the bank below, killed by the snake she trod on in her flight. In the seventeenth century, although the idea that a painting should show a single moment

Cat. no. 7 Joachim Wtewael (1566–1638), *The Judgement of Paris*
1615, oil on wood, 59.8 × 79.2 cm
London, National Gallery

For Junius, where a writer is forced to move from event to event in their proper order, a painter 'thrusteth himselfe into the very middest' choosing the principal moment of the story 'where it most concerneth him' as the focus of the painting and indicating events both past and future elsewhere: 'he maketh his Art all at once represent things alreadie done, things that are adoing, and things which are as yet to be done.' Having positioned his 'principall figures' in the 'principall place' the artist was to dispose the other scenes 'unto severall places, representing them a farre off in smaller figures, and sometimes also involving them and shutting them up as it were in a certaine kinde of mist … that they might rather resemble things alreadie done, than things that are a doing.'[18]

ALL AT ONCE

In Wtewael's *Judgement of Paris*, although it is not immediately apparent, the three goddesses and the messenger god Mercury all appear twice, in foreground and background. This is characteristic of continuous narrative, and it is often the repetition of a figure, usually wearing the same distinctive clothes, that alerts us to the fact that we are looking at separate rather than simultaneous events. But the repetition of individual characters is not essential for two moments separate in time to be combined within a single painting. Subsidiary scenes of subsequent or preceding events can feature a different cast to that of the principal scene, although the aim is then often less to tell a particular story than to provide a specific gloss upon it. It is a device

Fig. 15 *Ulysses and Polyphemus*, Spartan black-figure cup, sixth century BC, diameter 21.4 cm, Paris, Bibliothèque Nationale de France

Fig. 16 Titian, *The Death of Actaeon*, c.1565, oil on canvas, 178.4 × 198.1 cm, London, National Gallery

sometimes used in Christian art to illustrate the important idea that the events of Christ's life redeemed, and were prefigured by, events in the Old Testament. This explains the inclusion of Adam and Eve being expelled from the Garden of Eden in the background of a number of paintings of the Annunciation, emphasising the idea that the Virgin

Mary was the 'New Eve' through whom Paradise might be regained.

There is another way in which artists have combined more than one event within a single image, usually called the 'simultaneous' or 'complementary' method. A much-cited example from the ancient world is the scene on a sixth-century BC Spartan cup showing Ulysses and the Cyclops (fig. 15).[19] In the story as recounted in Homer's *Odyssey*, the Cyclops traps Ulysses and his companions in his cave, eating one of them each night. Ulysses gives the Cyclops wine that sends him to sleep, and then puts out his single eye with a burning log. On the cup these events are rendered as a single scene, in which the Cyclops holds the legs of a half-devoured Greek while Ulysses proffers a cup (which the Cyclops has no free hand to take) and, with his followers, drives a stick into the Cyclops's eye all apparently at the same time.

The supposedly primitive nature of the 'simultaneous method' has meant that it has not received much attention in discussions of later painting, but its principles have been of enormous importance for narrative painting. Uccello's *Saint George and the Dragon* (cat. no. 8), painted in the mid-fifteenth century, is pictorially considerably more sophisticated than the Spartan cup, but its treatment of narrative time is identical.[20] For those ignorant of the story (or of the reputation and habits of dragons) the picture would appear to show a knight on a white horse plunging his spear into the mouth of a pet dragon being taken for a walk by an elegant princess. In fact two separate incidents of Saint George's legend have been combined: firstly the dragon's wounding and secondly its humiliation – being tied to the princess's girdle to be led back to the city it had been terrorising.

The self-evident illogicalities of the Spartan cup or Uccello's *Saint George* are perhaps rare in painting, but the way in which they combine different moments in time within a single image is not. One common technique is to crowd a painting with separate incidents which, although related to its principal subject, could not have happened simultaneously. Crowded Crucifixion scenes often depict within a single space all or most of the episodes described in the Gospels and elsewhere as

Cat. no. 8 Paolo Uccello (1397–1475). *Saint George and the Dragon*
About 1460. oil on canvas. 56.5 × 74 cm
London, National Gallery

taking place around the central event: soldiers cast lots for Jesus's clothes; the centurion recognises Christ as the Son of God; the Virgin faints; the legs of the thieves are broken; the meaning of the event is discussed, and so on. Such scenes are not obviously contradictory as no figure is repeated and it would be possible for a group of people to be doing all these things simultaneously; but the Gospel accounts make it clear they did not.

Another related technique is to show cause and effect within a single image. blurring the temporal distinction between the two. In Titian's painting of *The Death of Actaeon* (fig. 16), we see Diana pursuing the figure of Actaeon, shown as half-man half-deer, as he is savaged by his own dogs. This is an ingenious illustration of the story in which Diana first curses Actaeon for spying on her, then splashes water onto his head thereby transforming him into a deer, after which he is ripped apart by his dogs. Here, rather than crowding the painting with references to separate elements of the story (as in the crowded Crucifixion scenes). Titian re-creates Ovid's gory tale by encompassing the whole story in a single scene; but not one that corresponds to any moment in the story as it was written.

THE FRUITFUL MOMENT
Both these approaches suggest a relaxed attitude towards both time and text. Surprisingly, both continued to be employed in the seventeenth century, when artists and theorists became increasingly preoccupied with the relationship between painting

Fig. 17 Carlo Maratti, *Apollo and Daphne*, 1681, oil on canvas,
221 × 224 cm, Brussels, Musées royaux des Beaux-Arts de Belgique

Fig. 18 Nicholas Poussin, *The Israelites gathering Manna*, 1639,
oil on canvas, 147 × 200 cm, Paris, Musée du Louvre

and time. From the Renaissance onwards, one of the difficulties for those wishing to establish a theory of painting had always been that no theoretical treatise on the subject survived from the ancient world. This was in marked contrast to the large body of surviving classical literary theory, most significantly the *Poetics* of Aristotle. However, in his *Ars Poetica*, Horace had famously declared '*ut pictura poesis*' – 'as painting so poetry' – apparently suggesting that the two art forms were equivalent and so encouraging the application of literary theory to painting.[21] One of

the most important planks of Aristotle's literary theory was that dramas should abide by what he termed the three 'unities' of action, time and place. In the most extreme interpretation of the unities, adopted by seventeenth-century dramatists, a drama was not only required to limit itself to a single story or 'action', but to be played out in a single setting and in real time – the events recounted taking as long as the play itself. Applying the theory of the unities to painting, critics increasingly insisted that a narrative painting should, indeed could, show only a single moment in time.

In this post-photographic age we are likely to think of a depicted 'moment' of a story as the equivalent of a snapshot, showing a split-second during the unfolding of an event. But this is not how most seventeenth-century critics thought of it. Writing in the 1690s the Italian critic Bellori extolled the virtues of a painting of *Apollo and Daphne* by the Italian Carlo Maratti (fig. 17), because it used a single pivotal moment to signify all the essential elements of the story.[22] But as in Titian's *Death of Actaeon*, Maratti's 'fruitful moment' did not correspond to any moment in Ovid's story. The painting not only includes Apollo and the fleeing Daphne sprouting laurel leaves, but also the hovering figure of Cupid, Daphne's father Peneus (to whom she prayed to be transformed) and a group of river gods and water nymphs. In Ovid's account these gods and nymphs later gather to console Peneus on the loss of his daughter and, in a telling phrase, Bellori describes their presence in the painting as an 'ingenious anachronism'. By including them as representatives of a future episode Maratti's painting encompasses the entire story but, crucially for Bellori, their presence is not awkward or illogical. Unlike a repeated figure, their presence does not manifestly contradict the idea that the painting represents a single moment in time, as it would if they had been shown already comforting a grieving Peneus before Daphne was fully transformed.

Another way the seventeenth-century definition of the moment in relation to paintings seems unlike the photographic model is suggested by a debate conducted at the French Academy in the 1660s. The debate followed a lecture by the Academy's President

Cat. no. 9 Paolo de Matteis (1622–1728), *The Choice of Hercules*
1712, oil on canvas, 64.1 × 76.8 cm
Leeds, Leeds Museums and Galleries, Temple Newsam

Charles Le Brun on Poussin's painting of *The Israelites gathering Manna* (fig. 18), painted some twenty-five years earlier. In a well-known letter Poussin had encouraged this picture's owner to 'read the story and the picture, so that you can judge whether everything is appropriate to its subject'.[23] The painting shows the full variety of reactions to the falling manna, including a striking group on the left of a woman breast-feeding her starving mother. It was on this group that the Academy debate concentrated, one member claiming it was not appropriate to the moment when the manna was falling and the Israelites were no longer hungry. Le Brun replied by acknowledging that unlike a writer

who can represent different actions successively to tell a story, the painter is more limited and 'has only one moment in which he has to take the object he wants to depict'. But he went on to excuse the presence of the group by suggesting that this moment might be extended:

> [The painter] sometimes has to combine many previous incidents to make us understand the subject he puts before us; without it his work would offer as little instruction to those who looked at it as the historian who, instead of telling his whole story, would just tell his end.[24]

Lord Shaftesbury banished this flexibility of the moment some fifty years later in his fascinating

Cat. no. 10 Rembrandt (1606–1669), *Belshazzar's Feast*
About 1636–8, oil on canvas, 167.6 × 209.2 cm
London, National Gallery

account of *The Choice of Hercules*, made on his instructions by Paolo de Matteis (cat. no. 9, previous page).[25] Shaftesbury complains about pictures where one cannot tell which of 'the distinct successive parts of the History or Action is that very-one represented':

> 'Tis evident, that every Master in Painting, when he has made choice of the determinate Date or Point of Time, according to which he wou'd represent his History, is afterwards debar'd the taking advantage from any other Action than what is immediately present, and belonging to that single instant he describes. For if he passes the present only for a moment, he may as well pass it for many years. And by this reckoning he may with as good right repeat the Same figure several times over …. To preserve therefore a just Conformity with historical Truth, and with the Unity of Time and Action, there remains no other way by which we can possibly give a hint of anything future, or call to mind anything past, than by setting in view such Passages or Events as have actually subsisted, or according to Nature might well subsist, or happen together in one and the same instant.

Here we have what appears to be the earliest theoretical insistence on painting as snapshot, so it is surprising to find that the picture produced on these principles has little sense of the instantaneous or momentary about it. Matteis's painting does not show an arrested moment of dramatic action, but a quieter one of transition. Faced with the story of the Judgement of Hercules (in which Hercules, called to choose between Virtue or Pleasure, eventually follows the path of Virtue) the artist could, according to Shaftesbury, choose one of three moments:

> Either ... the instant when the two Goddesses, VIRTUE and PLEASURE accost HERCULES; or when they are enter'd on their Dispute; Or when their Dispute is already far Advanc'd, and VIRTUE seems to gain her Cause.

It is the last of these that he recommends, the turning point when Hercules 'agonizes and with all his Strength of Reason endeavours to overcome himself'. Of the different moments this is 'the only one of the three, which can well serve to express the grand Event or consequent Resolution of HERCULES and the Choice he actually made'. In choosing the turning point in the story the artist can imply both what has past and the story's resolution. To the problem of 'How is it possible ... to express a Change of Passion in any Subject, since this Change is made by Succession' Shaftesbury offers two solutions. In the first place, because the 'Body moves slower than the mind' the body can reveal the figure's past disposition – and in Matteis's painting Hercules's body is turned towards Pleasure as his troubled face turns towards Virtue. The other possibility was for the artist 'to leave still in his Subject the Traces or Footsteps' of their previous emotion, 'for instance, when the plain Tracts of Tears new fallen, with other fresh tokens of Mourning and Dejection, remain still in a Person newly transported with Joy at the sight of a Relation or Friend, who the moment before had been lamented as one deces'd or lost'.

Shaftesbury's arguments were taken up by others in the eighteenth century and were given their most famous and influential formulation by the German writer and critic Gotthold Lessing in his *Laocoön*, first published in 1766.[26] Lessing's essay challenged the theory of '*ut pictura poesis*', emphasising the contrasts between the spheres of poetry and painting. For Lessing the defining difference lay in their respective relationship to time, and the fact that unlike poetry, painting could represent only 'a single moment of an action'. But this was not painting's only limitation: the choice of moment was also

restricted and, for a number of related reasons, it could not be one of emotional extreme. For the painted moment to be as effective as possible, for Lessing it needed to leave room for the imagination of the viewer and 'in the full course of an emotion no point is less suitable for this than its climax ... to present the utmost to the eye is to bind the wings of fancy'. The requirements of classical beauty also meant the artist should avoid moments of extreme emotion 'which are expressed by the most hideous contortions of the face and which throw the whole body into such unnatural positions as to lose all the beautiful contours of its natural state'. Finally Lessing believed that the single moment 'if it is to receive immutable permanence from art must express nothing transitory'. Just as Shaftesbury's insistence on the painting of a single recognisable moment had not resulted in a picture of arrested action, so Lessing argued that although some phenomena were 'sudden in their beginning and end', these should not be prolonged in art. Any frozen momentary action would, according to Lessing, appear increasingly unnatural the longer one looked at it.

In his desire to avoid the transient, Lessing was following classical academic thinking. But he was also implicitly rejecting a type of Baroque narrative painting that in all other ways meets his theoretical insistence on the single moment. It is a kind of painting exemplified by Rembrandt's *Belshazzar's Feast* (cat. no. 10), painted in the 1630s, in which everything suggests a split-second instant.[27] The Babylonian king is off balance having just leapt to his feet, sending guests and goblets flying. His eyes bulge with terror as he stares at the glowing writing that – he will learn – spells the end of his life and of his kingdom. His neighbours gape at him not yet aware of the cause of his distress. This is a snapshot vision that we are familiar with, but which was painted long before photography made such a way of seeing natural – or even possible. Rembrandt probably chose his subject precisely because of the opportunity it offered to depict a moment of extreme emotional intensity. The Bible text (Daniel 5:6) itself focuses attention on the suddenness of Belshazzar's change of mood and his emotional turmoil: 'Then the king's countenance was changed, and his thoughts

Fig. 19 Caravaggio, *The Supper at Emmaus*, 1601, oil and egg on canvas, 141 × 196.2 cm, London, National Gallery

troubled him, so that the joints of his loins were loosed and his knees smote against another', and Rembrandt's intention was clearly to depict the split-second instant as carefree carousing turned to abject terror. Rembrandt, famed for his ability to depict intense and conflicting emotions, often focussed on dramatic reversals that allowed him to encompass a story in the blink of an eye. The falling goblets emphasise this suddenness, and Rembrandt used this device elsewhere. In his painting of the sacrifice of Isaac, a falling dagger performs this same role when, on the very brink of sacrificing his son, Abraham is prevented by the angel.

One of Rembrandt's most important predecessors in the desire to capture the extreme momentary expression was Caravaggio, whose *Supper at Emmaus* (fig. 19), painted in Rome nearly forty years before *Belshazzar's Feast*, depicts another instant of sudden reversal in which the two disciples recognise with astonishment that their fellow diner is the risen Christ. In Caravaggio's *Boy Bitten by a Lizard* (cat. no. 11), painted slightly earlier the subject of the painting seems to be the momentary expression

itself.[28] There have, it is true, been numerous (conflicting) allegorical interpretations proposed for the painting, but since it was painted for sale, rather than to commission, it is unlikely that it had an elaborate iconographic structure. The earliest account of the painting, written in 1642, describes it purely in terms of expression, 'you could almost hear the boy scream',[29] and it seems likely that Caravaggio's main concern was to demonstrate his skill in capturing the boy's shock and pain. Just as in *Belshazzar's Feast*, it is the extreme nature of the expression that marks it as momentary, but so too do other details: the unbalanced pose; the rising spray of drapery to the right of the face, and the dangling, squirming lizard itself. All these elements cannot possibly remain as they are, and so carry with them the promise of future movement. It is this that gives the impression that we are looking at a frozen instant. It is, in other words, movement that defines the moment.

Cat. no. 11 Caravaggio (1571–1610), *Boy Bitten by a Lizard*
1595–1600, oil on canvas, 66 × 49.5 cm
London, National Gallery

Moment and Movement

DEPICTING MOVEMENT in still images presents the artist with as many problems as the depiction of narrative. In this photographic age we are familiar with images of bodies frozen in motion, and have perhaps lost the capacity to be surprised by them, except in extreme cases such as Harold Edgerton's photographs of bullets captured in mid-flight (fig. 20).[1] Reactions to early snapshot photographs in the 1850s, 60s and 70s, when for the first time faster emulsions and shutter speeds allowed photographs to capture bodies in motion, reveal an amazement towards images that we would now take for granted. The photographs were described as 'instantaneous', but the term is misleading if not meaningless: in the late 1850s the fastest exposure time was about one-tenth of a second. Contemporary responses to these snapshots differed markedly in tone, but all accepted that they revealed a world never seen before – a fact seen as of particular import for artists. On the one hand 'instantaneous photographs' were proclaimed as a revelation providing artists 'with the true attitudes of movement, those positions of the body in unstable balance for which no model can pose'.[2] But elsewhere it was argued that photography presented a false vision of movement that failed to take the limitations of sight into account. In an article accompanied by illustrations taken from photographs of walking figures, the American author O.W. Holmes commented tellingly that 'no artist would have dared to draw a walking figure in attitudes like some of these'.[3]

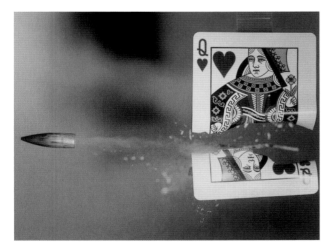

Fig. 20 Harold Edgerton, *Queen of Hearts Playing Card hit by a 0.3 calibre bullet*, 1970, photograph, London, The Victoria and Albert Museum

SEEING MOVEMENT

The different responses reflect the same fact: that the movements documented by photographs were not those familiar from painting. In some cases photographs even revealed that painters sometimes failed to observe movement accurately. Most famously the first photographs to capture the horse in motion, published in 1878 by Eadweard Muybridge (fig. 21), revealed that only one of the four attitudes in which European art had traditionally shown galloping horses was correct, and that that one – visible on the Parthenon frieze – had not been used since ancient Greece. Muybridge made much capital from this point during his triumphant lecture tour to Paris and London in 1881–2 as reported in an entertaining account of his London lectures:

> Not the least instructive part of his lecture was his contrast between the positions of animals shown in ancient and modern art with their true positions

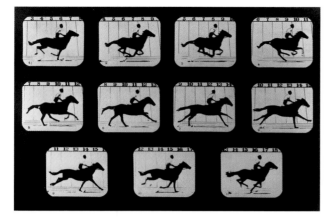

Fig. 21 Eadweard Muybridge, *Sallie Gardner Running*, 1878, toned cyanotype, Stanford, Iris and B. Gerald Cantor Center for Visual Arts at Stanford University, Muybridge Collection

Fig. 22 Titian, *Bacchus and Ariadne*, 1522–3, oil on canvas, 175.2 × 190.5 cm, London, National Gallery

as shown by themselves in presence of the camera. The audience listened calmly enough while Egyptian, Assyrian, Roman and Renaissance artists were put out of court … But Mr Muybridge next showed a photograph from an English picture of a racehorse at full speed, with his four legs extended to the utmost limit, and his feet off the ground. He pointed out that the position was impossible, and that if once the animal got into it he would infallibly break his back in coming down. A moment later appeared a photograph of ten such horses; 'all as you see,' observed Mr Muybridge, 'exactly like the first horse and each other. If it be impossible for one horse to assume such an attitude, to find ten horses doing it all at once would be nothing short of a miracle.' This remark the audience applauded, upon which the lecturer added with delusive calmness: 'The ten impossible horses as you see them are photographed from Mr Frith's well-known picture of *The Derby Day*.' The audience shuddered. At least half of them must have been in the habit of regarding Frith's *Derby Day* as among the triumphs of modern art …. At the Royal Academy this passage was necessarily suppressed.[4]

The response of artists to these revelations was unsurprisingly mixed. At one extreme the French Academic painter Meissonier allegedly exclaimed 'If I could only repaint Friedland', his huge battle canvas of 1875, before producing a watercolour version in 1887 that corrected some of the 'errors' revealed by Muybridge's photographs.[5] But others insisted on the expressive truth of conventional representation of movement. This was a position maintained in the early twentieth century by the sculptor Auguste Rodin who objected to the very idea of photographic 'truth' when talking of his statue of the walking (flat-footed) John the Baptist:

It is the artist who is truthful and it is photography which lies, for in reality time does not stop, and if the artist succeeds in producing the impression of movement which takes several moments for the accomplishment, his work is certainly much less conventional than the scientific image, where time is abruptly suspended.[6]

Without the aid of photography, every stage of a movement may not be visible. But some phases of it are more memorably perceived than others, and it is these that the painter usually depicts. These are usually when the direction of the movement changes: a pendulum, for example, will be most visible at the top of its swing. In the same way, to take Holmes's and Rodin's undramatic example, walking legs are most clearly seen between strides, just before the back leg swings forward, and artists have made this the conventional 'walking pose' in paintings. In Titian's *Bacchus and Ariadne* (fig. 22), Ariadne on the left, the young foreground faun, the Bacchante

Fig. 23 El Greco. *Christ driving the Traders from the Temple* (detail), c.1600, oil on canvas, 106 × 129.7 cm, London, National Gallery

Fig. 24 Bernardo Cavallino, *Christ driving the Traders from the Temple* (detail), 1645–50, oil on canvas, 101 × 127.6 cm, London, National Gallery

Fig. 25 Paolo Veronese, *Allegory of Love, II* (detail), probably 1570s, oil on canvas, 186.6 × 188.5 cm, London, National Gallery

Fig. 26 Style of Bonifazio, *The Labours of the Months* (detail), early 16th century, oil on canvas, each 13.3 × 10.2 cm, London, National Gallery

brandishing her cymbals and the man battling with writhing snakes are all walking in step – the toes of their right feet all about to leave the ground and swing forward. It was the intermediate phases of walking revealed by photography that were considered so surprising, ungainly and illegible. It is not only walking legs which are usually painted at the moment of fullest extension: the cymbals of Titian's Bacchante are at the top of their swing, and the raised foot of the satyr at the extreme right is, we anticipate, about to be brought down with a stamp. Our tendency to anticipate motion allows artists to give the impression of movement as we naturally interpret a raised foot or fist, hammer or whip, as about to come down. Moreover, we read it as at the top of its swing, rather than on its descent or ascent (figs. 23–6). The other extreme of a hammer blow – when it hits its mark – is in contrast hardly ever painted, as without any clue as to the force of its downward swing, the hammer will appear to rest on the surface rather than hitting it.

Movements are represented most convincingly at the top of their swing, and that moment also has the secondary advantage – for the artist's model – of being for the most part the easiest to hold as a pose. It is far easier to brandish a sword, whip or hammer as if about to strike than to attempt to freeze the motion halfway through a downward blow or upward thrust. But this fact carries with it the danger

that these attitudes, when painted, will indeed look posed. This was the source of one of the criticisms levelled against Caravaggio by a number of his earliest critics, arising from his reported boast that he would only paint directly from the model. Giulio Mancini, writing around 1620, complained of the impossibility of assembling in a room groups of figures 'having to laugh or cry or pretending to walk while having to stay still in order to be copied. As a result the figures, though they look forceful, lack movement, expression and grace'.[7] This may seem an odd criticism to level at the artist of the dynamic *Boy Bitten by a Lizard* (cat. no. 11), but it is altogether more understandable when one looks to some of his narrative paintings. Even *The Supper at Emmaus* (fig. 19), despite the apparent emphasis on the momentary, has something of a tableau about it. There is no pose here that cannot be held, no one is off balance or toppling. Where Rembrandt showed goblets falling, Caravaggio's fruit basket, though precarious, remains standing. As one writer has neatly put it. Caravaggio's figures are often 'merely going through the motions of movement'.[8]

It is the degree to which a pose is unstable that gives the clearest indication of movement. In Leonardo da Vinci's surviving writings on the movement of the human body, his constant emphasis is on the body's centre of gravity, and the ways in which movement sends a figure off balance: 'The faster a man runs, the more he leans forward towards the point he runs to and throws more weight in front of his axis than behind.'[9] This certainly accords with the conventional representations of running figures – leaning forward, often flinging both arms before them – but it has more to do with artistic convention than the more accurate upright posture of runners. An obviously off-balance figure will lead a viewer to anticipate and supply their future movement. Alternatively where the pose itself does not provide this information, clothes can perform the same function. Using drapery to suggest or augment the sense of movement is an invaluable artistic tool. To return to *Bacchus and Ariadne*, the boy faun's cape, and the dresses of the the Bacchantes and Ariadne all rise behind them to suggest their forward momentum; but none do so as obviously or to such an extreme as Bacchus's cloak which flies out behind him as he leaps from his chariot. Bacchus is not wearing his cloak; it is there only to describe his leap. The flying cloak or trailing scarf or belt is so familiar in painting that its conventional nature is easy to overlook. The flying cloak can be seen as the direct predecessor of the 'speed lines' of the cartoonist and graphic artist – and it is no accident that so many comic book superheroes are caped crusaders.

FALLING FIGURES

While Bacchus's cloak describes his movement, it is the fact that he is depicted in mid-leap that emphasises the scene's 'splendid suddenness'.[10] A leaping or falling figure is an extreme example of a pose that presupposes a split second captured, but even a cursory comparison of falling figures in paint and print shows that some falls last longer than others – and that the duration of a painted moment depends on more than movement alone.

When faced with a falling figure we mentally fast forward to the moment of impact, and our sense of the snatched moment depends in part on how imminent this is. This is surely one of the reasons why Crespi's print of the mischievous and foolish Bertoldino – a figure of popular Italian literature – plummeting towards a fish pond after a disastrous flying experiment, is so successful in suggesting the frozen instant before splashdown (cat. no. 12).[11] In

Fig. 27 Hendrik Goltzius, after Cornelis van Haarlem, *Ixion*, 1588, engraving, diameter 32.2 cm, London, The British Museum

contrast, one might point to the curious calm of the tumbling figure of Phaeton, from the series known as *The Four Disgracers* engraved by Hendrick Goltzius after a design by Cornelis van Haarlem (cat. no. 13, overleaf).[12] All four prints in this impressive series show falling mythological figures, Phaeton, Icarus, Tantalus and Ixion, each cast down by the gods for their overarching ambition. Here the inscription warns that 'overly rash desires lead to bad ends', a suitable lesson to accompany Phaeton, who stole and lost control of Apollo's sun chariot (shown falling in the distance), before being flung from it by Zeus's thunderbolt. Cornelis's choice of subjects seems influenced less by a desire for split-second drama than by the opportunities the falling body offered for involved and ingenious figural compositions. The series was made at a time when, according to his earliest biographer, he was particularly concerned with the varieties of pose possible with the nude figure, and the poses of the series as a whole are carefully and ingeniously balanced. Two are viewed from the back, two from the front, two fall head down, two head up. The poses are also matched in pairs – Phaeton's is essentially the same as Ixion's viewed in reverse (fig. 27). Looking at the prints as a series we seem to circle around a single suspended

Si rompe la Cintura, e in giù profonda,
Forse per ripescare il suo Ceruello
Jcaro Bertoldin dentro de l'Onda.

Cat. no. 12 Giuseppe Maria Crespi (1665–1747), *Bertoldino Falling into the Fishpond*
About 1710, etching, 20.3 × 14.2 cm
London, The British Museum

Cat. no. 13 Hendrik Goltzius (1558–1617) after Cornelis van Haarlem, *Phaeton*
1588, engraving, diameter 32.2 cm
London, The British Museum

figure, and in looking at each print we are encouraged to turn it around as we read the inscriptions on the circular frame. It is not entirely surprising that the series acquired the unflattering nickname of 'the somersaulters'.

The surprising absence of a sense of plummeting movement in Goltzius's print is not only because Phaeton has so far to fall, but also because of the way in which he has been depicted. Each muscle and lock of elegantly rising hair has been carefully and painstakingly described – in marked contrast to the apparently swiftly and economically drawn figure of Crespi's Bertoldino. The elaboration of the detail somehow militates against the impression of movement which, experience tells us, is more easily obtained with a few swift, dynamic strokes than by

Cat. no. 14 Johann Liss (about 1595–1626/30), *The Fall of Phaeton*
About 1624, oil on canvas, 128 × 110 cm
London, National Gallery

Cat. no. 15 David Hockney (1937–), *Picture Emphasising Stillness*
1962, oil and letraset on canvas, 153 × 180 cm
Lisbon, Colecção Berardo – Sintra Museu de Arte Moderna

meticulous rendering. This fact is easier to state than to explain. It must depend in part on the difficulty of distinguishing the details of objects in rapid motion, a phenomenon apparently contradicted by overly detailed images (an issue which, as we shall see, was addressed in the seventeenth century with regard to spinning-wheel spokes). As important, however, is our awareness of the speed of the work's execution itself, which seems able to endow an image with motion. The evident movement and sensed swiftness of a brushstroke or pen mark – often in the same direction as the depicted movement – somehow transfers itself onto the object represented.

In Johann Liss's *Fall of Phaeton* (cat. no. 14, previous page), probably painted in about 1624 when the German-born artist was in Rome or Venice, the falling figure in the sky is deliberately indistinct. His head is turned away and his flesh tones and red cloak are taken up in the surrounding clouds.[13] But, as in Goltzius's *Four Disgracers*, there is little sense of the instant captured. Liss has extended the narrative: he includes Phaeton's grieving sisters; the winged Heliades, god of the river Eridanus into which Phaeton fell; and the group of grieving nymphs on the left. In each case there is evident concentration on the momentary expressions and gestures of grief and dismay, emphasised in the group of nymphs by the billowing – and now much darkened – drapery above them. But the inclusion of different groups, each of which has to be taken in by the viewer, does not help any sense of the instantaneous. Linked to this is the fact that Phaeton falls in the distance. Experience tells us, whether we are looking from the window of a speeding train or standing on the edge of a racetrack, that the relative motion of objects near to us appears more rapid than those far away. This is a phenomenon known as motion parallax, and means that a falling figure in the distance will actually seem to fall more slowly than one near to us. The same phenomenon explains why both Rembrandt and Caravaggio chose a dramatic close-up for their scenes of arrested motion. Proximity contributes to the sense of the instant.

Depicting a figure falling in space, although inevitably suggesting motion at the same time, can also draw attention to the stillness of the depiction itself – and indeed to the limitations of the still image in conveying movement. The faster the movement the more aware one is of its freezing, for we never actually see plummeting objects suspended in midair. The point was neatly made by David Hockney in one of the paintings he made in the early 1960s exploring the limitations of the painted image. Called *Picture Emphasising Stillness* (cat. no. 15), it shows a male couple apparently about to be flattened by a huge leopard.[14] Like Bacchus the leopard is in mid-leap and although he does not have a flying cloak, the trailing clouds above him perform a similar function. Indeed the choice of a leopard, Bacchus's beast, might even suggest a nod towards Titian's painting. But Hockney's leopard will never reach his prey; between them is written the sly sentence: 'They are perfectly safe: this is a still.'

BLUR

Every painting is a 'still', but painters' attempts to depict motion have not been limited merely to freezing figures and objects in attitudes or positions of action. As we have seen, one of the objections to the snapshot as it developed in the 1860s and 70s was that it showed phases of a movement that were normally invisible. The Frenchman Eugène Véron,

writing in 1878, saw instantaneous photography as anathema since, according to the theory of the persistence of vision (which addresses the continued visual perception of an object in a given location even though its image no longer falls on that part of the retina), we never see instants of immobility, but rather perceive motion as a fluid blurred movement. He wrote that 'Photography doesn't give movement precisely because it only seizes fixed attitudes … the first obligation of art is to accommodate the physiological conditions of humanity'.[15] Véron was not alone; some ten years later the American W. de. W. Abney made essentially the same point in an article called 'Are instantaneous photographs true?'. Again his objection was that such images failed to take into account the limits of normal vision: his specific objection being that photographs of spinning-wheels showed every spoke when they were actually perceived as a blur.[16]

The history of the blur in painting is fascinating and in many ways surprising. The theory of the persistence of vision was certainly not new to the nineteenth century – Ptolemy in the second century had referred to the invisibility of the spokes of a rapidly turning wheel. Among Leonardo da Vinci's observations of the visible world are a number of descriptions of similar phenomena: he notes that a vibrating knife blade or lute string will appear doubled;[17] that 'the droplets of rain descending from the clouds appear as a continuous line, demonstrating how the eye holds the impression of the moving thing it sees';[18] and elsewhere that 'every object that moves with speed seems to tinge its path with the semblance of its colour … if you move a lighted brand with a circular motion it will appear that its whole course is a flaming circle'.[19] Leonardo also observed the way in which one can see through a spinning-wheel:

Actual motion made with rapid impetus will never obstruct from the eye the object which is behind the body that is moving … as happens with the motion of certain instruments worked by women, made for the purpose of gathering their threads together … for these by their circular motion are so swift that through being perforated they do not obstruct to the eye anything behind them.[20]

Despite these observations Leonardo does not suggest that these phenomena be painted in this way. The diagrams accompanying his writings illustrate his observations, but there are no blurred wheels or lute strings in his paintings. Throughout the fifteenth and sixteenth centuries wheels were shown with each spoke clearly delineated (fig. 28), and it was not until the seventeenth century that Western painters first painted them as blurred. The most famous example is Velázquez's extraordinarily effective depiction of the stroboscopic effect of a spinning-wheel in his painting of the fable of Arachne, known as *Las Hilanderas* (fig. 29).[21]

The Dutch painter Philips Angel addressed the problem of depicting wheels in motion sixteen years before Velázquez's painting in a speech delivered to his fellow artists in Leiden in 1641.[22] He complained that wheels in paintings always appear still, and argued that artists:

> Could have avoided this error if they had paid closer attention to the natural movement, presenting us with the form as it truly appears, for whenever a cartwheel or a spinning-wheel is turned with great force one sees that, because of the rapid rotation, no spokes are really seen but only an uncertain shimmer of them, yet although I have seen many pictures in which carriage wheels are depicted, I have never seen this imitated properly,

Fig. 29 Velázquez, *Las Hilanderas* (detail), 1657, oil on canvas, 167 × 252 cm, Madrid, Museo Nacional del Prado

but with each spoke drawn or painted in such a way that the carriage did not appear to move, such that there was no distinction between a stationary carriage and one that was supposedly in motion. Angel was a modest painter and no great theoretician, but he was apparently the first to draw attention to the problem of representing, rather than perceiving, a turning wheel, although he does not exactly propose a solution and, as far as we know, did not attempt to find one in his own paintings. He may have been prompted in this direction by his reading of the first-century Roman author Pliny who, in his biography of the classical painter Aristides, described paintings of carriages 'so life-like … that one would swear that the wheels turned and rolled along'.[23] Whether this lay behind Angel's observation or not, his comments seem to have concentrated the minds of his contemporaries. Nicolaes Maes, one of Rembrandt's pupils, may well have been directly responding to Angel's challenge in his *Woman Spinning* (cat. no. 16), probably painted about fourteen years after Angel's speech, and slightly earlier than Velázquez's painting.[24] It seems also that Maes was not alone in his response. Another of Rembrandt's pupils, Samuel van Hoogstraten, writing in the 1670s, refers to a painting by the Leiden artist Gerrit Dou of a 'whirling spinning-wheel', comparing it directly to Aristides's carriages in which 'the wheels appear to turn'.[25]

It would not be surprising if Pliny's account of Aristides's turning wheels played some part in the

Fig. 28 Agostino Veneziano, *Phaeton* (detail), 1516–36, engraving, 22.3 × 13.9 cm, London, British Museum

Cat. no. 16 Nicolaes Maes (1634–1693), *Woman Spinning*
About 1655, oil on canvas, 63 × 55 cm
Amsterdam, Rijksmuseum

Cat. no. 17 George Stubbs (1724–1806), *Phaeton and the Horses of the Sun*
1762, oil on canvas, 97.8 × 121.9 cm
Saltram, The Morley Collection, National Trust

conception and execution of Stubbs's painting of
Phaeton and its depiction of hurtling speed
(cat. no. 17).[26] This is Phaeton before his fall, running
out of control in the chariot of the sun and about to
be flung from it by Zeus's thunderbolt. It was a very
significant painting for Stubbs, the first he exhibited in
public at the Society of Artists, and of a subject he was
to paint a number of times. With it he clearly wished to
show that an animal painter could also turn his hand
to the more elevated genre of history painting. The
subject was, of course, carefully chosen to lend itself
to his particular skill. Ovid's text describes Phaeton's
horses running 'uncontrolled where-e'er their Fury
drove', and the extraordinary group of madly galloping

horses, one of which is biting the neck of its neighbour,
is certainly the painting's most impressive passage.
Beside the drama of the maddened team of horses the
figure of Phaeton himself, leaning back to rein them in,
is curiously ineffectual; but the same cannot be said of
his chariot. Indeed it is the chariot's wheels, painted all
ablur and with flames and smoke streaming from their
axles, that suggest hurtling speed most effectively.

Stubbs's intention was clearly to present as
convincing an impression of speed as he was able.
About 100 years later Turner turned his very different
means to the same ends in *Rain Steam and Speed*
(cat. no. 18).[27] The title of his painting, which shows a
locomotive hurtling across the Thames at Maidenhead,

makes his intention entirely clear and Thackeray, writing in *Fraser's Magazine* made much of his success:

> As for Mr Turner, he has out-prodigied all former prodigies … there comes a train down upon you, really moving at the rate of 50 miles an hour, and which the reader had best make haste to see, lest it should dash out of the picture, and be away up Charing Cross through the wall opposite.[28]

Although struck by the effect, Thackeray was not prepared to speculate on how it was achieved, 'as for the manner in which the "Speed" is done, of that the less said the better'. This sentiment was shared by the reviewer of the *Morning Chronicle* who wrote 'how these wonderful effects are produced is beyond the power of man to say'.[29] Others did attempt to explain the success of one of the first truly effective images of speed. Charles Eastlake, Director of the National Gallery, suggested in 1857 that 'the indication of speed was marked by three puffs of steam, the nearest to the engine being of course the most distinct, the other two gradually less so',[30] which although based on an accurate observation is clearly inadequate as an explanation. George Leslie, who as a nine-year-old, watched Turner put the finishing touches to the painting before its exhibition at the Royal Academy in 1844, suggested even less convincingly that the *Speed* of the title referred to the hare, which he saw Turner add to the painting, scampering in front of the hurtling locomotive.[31]

But the basis of the illusion of speed is surely Turner's ingenious manipulation of the blur, or what he called its 'indistinctness'. Painting the

Cat. no. 18 Joseph Mallord William Turner (1775–1851). *Rain, Steam and Speed – The Great Western Railway*
Before 1844, oil on canvas, 90.8 × 121.9 cm
London, National Gallery

atmospheric effects of extreme weather conditions was part of Turner's stock in trade, and *Rain, Steam and Speed* is not his only 'indistinct' painting, but against this hazy atmosphere, the silhouette of the black-funnelled locomotive is delineated with razor-sharp exactness. This is the reverse of what we might expect; it is not the moving object that is blurred but its surroundings. This blurring has been seen as evoking scenery as seen from a speeding railway carriage, which might explain the longevity of the familiar (but questionable) story describing the painting as directly inspired by a train journey that Turner took in similarly wild conditions.[32] But Turner's 'indistinctness' is atmospheric rather than the result of movement. The rushing train, darker and more distinct than anything else, is projected forward in aerial perspective – its clarity makes it appear closer. The device succeeds because the train is rushing towards us and not running parallel to the picture plane. The sharp focus of the train may be a response to two other characteristics of our perception of motion as well. On the one hand it reflects the extraordinarily strong visual appeal exerted by motion. We automatically turn our attention towards moving objects, and Turner's engine in its clarity and tone, as well as its flash of red, may attract our eye in a comparable way. It also reflects the way we actually look at moving objects – tracking them using what psychologists call the 'smooth pursuit' mechanism. This causes the background to move relative to the eye while the image of the object itself is stabilised; in other words when we look at a moving body, it is the background that blurs as the object itself is held in sharp focus.

THE BLUR AND THE PHOTOGRAPH

Just as photography dramatically altered attitudes towards depictions of the frozen moment, it has also altered perception of blurred images. The blur in photography is both a common menace for the incompetent snapper and a conventional indicator of movement. The blurring of fast-moving objects – be they wheel spokes or lute strings – is a visual phenomena that was observed long before the invention of photography, but photographic blur could describe the movement of even the most sluggish object and so greatly extended the blur's expressive potential.

The slow exposure times of early photography meant that moving objects could not be captured at all. The earliest photographs of urban scenes are eerily depopulated, with only the occasional ghost of some figure or carriage that had paused long enough to register on the photographic plate. As exposure times shortened people began to appear as insubstantial shapes dragging smears behind them or, as in one particularly fine daguerreotype of cavalry troops entering the Place de la Concorde, as a blurred river of motion (fig. 30). Photographers and critics alike complained of the new medium's inability to capture movement, and technology advanced with remarkable rapidity towards faster shutter speeds and emulsions until the development of the 'instantaneous' photograph during the 1860s and 70s. But while the efforts of pioneers were directed towards shortening exposure times, some painters (and photographers) recognised the expressive possibilities of the photographic blur. The smeared figures of the crowd in Monet's two paintings of the *Boulevard des Capucines* of 1873 (fig. 31) are much-cited examples.[33] The link with photography seems inescapable, but Monet himself never acknowledged the debt and no contemporary critic suggested a connection – even though most commented on the unconventional, and for some illegible, representation

Fig. 30 Francois A. Certes, *Parade at the Place de la Concorde, Paris*, c.1848, daguerreotype, 21.9 × 27.8 cm, Los Angeles, J. Paul Getty Museum

of the crowd. The critic Chesneau did, however, relate their appearance to their movement:

> Never has the amazing animation of the public thoroughfare, the ant-like swarming of the crowd on the pavement and the vehicles on the roadway, the movement of the trees in the dust and light along the boulevard; never has the elusive, the fleeting, the instantaneity of the movement been caught in its incredible flux, and fixed, as it is in this extraordinary ... *Boulevard des Capucines*.[34]

Some twenty years later, in 1891, the Norwegian artist Edvard Munch painted a scene of the *Rue de Rivoli* in Paris (cat. no. 19, overleaf) using the language of the photographic blur far more explicitly to suggest the traffic of the street.[35] Here, blurred smears and dragged brush strokes describe carriages changing lanes or turning corners and hurrying crowds in a way that would have been entirely illegible to viewers before the photograph. It would not be surprising if Munch had been looking at early photographs: the medium had celebrated its fiftieth anniversary in 1889 and Munch used photographs as inspiration and tool throughout his career. The previous year he had based *Spring Day on Karl Johan Street*, another street scene set in his native Christiana (now Oslo), on a picture postcard. The central figures in that painting, although not blurred in the manner of the *Rue de Rivoli*, are curiously transparent in a manner akin to the ethereal half-captured figures in early photographs.

The subject of the *Rue de Rivoli* clearly pays homage to Munch's Impressionist predecessors, including Monet, Pissarro and Caillebotte, and Munch himself described the motif as 'typically French'. Its curious use of short divided diagonal brush marks also reveals the more recent influence of the divisionism or pointillist technique of artists such as Seurat. In the painting's emphasis on the impression of movement, Munch may have been attempting to explore, and move beyond, what was seen as one of the principal characteristics of Impressionism. The idea of Impressionism that filtered through to Norway in the 1880s was a partial one but, as expounded in an article of 1882 by Munch's contemporary and friend Erik Werenskiold,

Fig. 31 Claude Monet, *Boulevard des Capucines*, 1873, oil on canvas, 80 × 60 cm, Kansas City, The Nelson Atkins Museum of Art

its primary objective was to capture the most ephemeral visual sensations. For Werenskiold one of the Impressionist's principal means in achieving this end was their use of the blur. His example is familiar:

> When a wheel turns, they do not paint each spoke, they are happy to indicate it. They try to emphasise the vibrating, the indistinct, the fleeting, that is to say whatever characterises movement.[36]

Although Munch was certainly responding to Impressionist precedent he later described his *Rue de Rivoli* as marking a break from his Impressionist phase. This is presumably in part a reference to the painting's divisionist technique, but it may also refer to his exaggerated depiction of movement. In the *Rue de Rivoli* he uses the blur far more emphatically than the Impressionists had ever done. Perhaps prompted by photography, he moved beyond merely recording visual sensation to what might be described as a symbolic use of the blur: an extended, worried smear of paint standing for the passage of a moving carriage.

Cat. no. 19 Edvard Munch (1863–1944). *Rue de Rivoli*
1891. oil on canvas. 79.7 × 64.5 cm
Cambridge. Mass.. The Fogg Art Museum. Harvard University Art Museums. gift of Rudolf Serkin

SEQUENTIAL MOVEMENT

The blurring of a form may help to suggest its simple directional movement, but it cannot describe any complex action. Artists have resorted to other means to represent sequences of movement, perhaps nowhere more elegantly than in Poussin's *A Bacchanalian Revel before a Term of Pan* (cat. no. 20).[37] Here, the interweaving and interlocking figures describe a single sinuous movement unfolding itself across the canvas 'with the ease and naturalness of a ribbon unfurling in the wind'.[38] All the characteristic devices to denote movement and moment are in place: raised feet and arms; billowing drapery; fluttering ribbons and hair; even suspended drops squeezed from the grapes of the nymph on the left. But the progress of the dance is also conveyed, and we read the continued movement of each figure into its neighbour as we move our eyes from one to the next.

The contrast between Poussin's harmonious yet sprightly dance and the wild cavorting depicted by Rubens in his *Peasant Dance* or *Kermis* (fig. 32), now in the Louvre, could scarcely be more marked. Where Poussin showed nymphs, fauns and sylvan boys, Rubens puts us in altogether earthier company – company that revolted the nineteenth-century critic Ruskin:

> A crowd of peasants near some place, drinking, dancing like baboons, hauling each other by the part of the body where a waist should be, kissing and – men and women alike – fighting for pots of beer.[39]

Here too, Rubens invites us to follow the stages of a movement: in the centre of the composition five spinning, kissing couples seem to show different phases of a single action – an action that reaches a resolution in the reclining couple kissing on the central axis beneath them. The sense of movement as

Cat. no. 20 Nicolas Poussin (1594–1665), *A Bacchanalian Revel before a Term of Pan*
1630–4, oil on canvas, 99.7 × 142.9 cm
London, National Gallery

Cat. no. 21 Rubens (1577–1640), *Seventeen Studies for a Pair of Dancers in a Village Festival*
1630–1, black and red chalk reworked in pen and ink, 58.2 × 50.2 cm
London, The British Museum

Fig. 32 Rubens, *Peasant Dance* or *Kermis*, c.1631–2, oil on panel, 149 × 261 cm, Paris, Musée du Louvre

described by a sequence of separate figures is even more evident in the extraordinary sheet of studies, drawn first in chalk and then in pen, that Rubens produced for the painting (cat. no. 21).[40] The sheet is worked on both sides: on one side are studies of disparate groups of figures drinking, sleeping, dancing and fighting, but on the other is drawn a single couple, their mouths locked together as they spin across and down the sheet, the rhythms of the dance echoed in the repetitions of Rubens's pen strokes. The effect of sequence produced by Rubens's drawing is, however, more apparent than real. Each pose does not lead to the next: the hands that are linked and raised change from couple to couple. It is, in fact, unlikely that Rubens was drawing from life as he seems to have been experimenting with varieties of pose, perhaps seeking the most dynamic and expressive. But in looking at the sheet our tendency to read the shifting images as showing temporal progression is hard to escape because of our familiarity with the notion of examining a movement 'frame' by 'frame' in photographic sequences.

The earliest photographic analyses of motion used the sequential presentation of parts of a

movement. There is a remarkable – if fortuitous – similarity between the format of Rubens's studies and the series of photographs of a rather more sedately spinning couple published by Muybridge in 1887 as one of the 781 plates in his eleven-volume *Animal Locomotion* (cat. no. 22, overleaf), an extraordinarily rich compendium of men, women and animals engaged in a wide range of actions.[41] Muybridge embarked on this ambitious project in 1883 with backing from the University of Pennsylvania. The University appointed a committee to ensure the work's 'thoroughly scientific character', but Muybridge often appears to have been more concerned with creating appealing, striking or intriguing narrative imagery than analytically verifiable data. His methods were also suspect: he used banks of cameras, usually in groups of twelve, each triggered separately. This made the accurate measurement of the intervals between each frame difficult – especially when cameras failed, as they often did. The fact that each 'still' was taken from a slightly different position (evident in the shifting perspective of the grid on which the spinning couple dance) would have further complicated any attempts

Cat. no. 22 Eadweard Muybridge (1830–1904), 'Dancing Couple' from *Animal Locomotion*
1887, collotype, 28.2 × 26.5 cm
London, The Victoria and Albert Museum

at analysis. Against these failings must be placed the extraordinary wealth of figurative imagery that Muybridge produced. His often naked subjects – university athletes, professional models, local workmen and, on occasion, himself – were put through a bewildering variety of paces. The resulting sequences of men and women, walking and running, jumping and throwing, wielding cricket bats and drinking cups of tea, making beds and pouring buckets of water over each other, are among the most memorable photographic images of the nineteenth century. Even the animals he photographed, both in his studio and at Philadelphia's Zoological Gardens, could find themselves involved in unexpected dramas: the final plate of *Animal Locomotion* was 'Chickens being Scared by a Torpedo'.

Muybridge's photographic sequences not only illustrated movement, they were used to synthesise it. From the time of his first experiments in the 1870s, Muybridge recognised the possibility of re-animating his images using one of the so-called 'philosophical toys', such as the phenakistoscope and zoetrope. These optical devices, believed to demonstrate the persistence of vision, give the illusion of movement by presenting a sequence of images to the viewer in rapid succession. The perceived movement is not, in fact, the result of visual persistence alone, but also depends upon the so-called phi-phenomenon. This is our inescapable tendency to 'fill the gaps' between successively presented images and to interpret their differences as being the result of motion – provided of course that the images relate closely enough to each other and are presented at the required rate. There is no such thing as a moving picture. When we watch a movie today we are actually watching a blank screen for about half the time, while a rapid sequence of still photographs, at the rate of 24 per second, are flashed on and off before our eyes. Muybridge himself developed a projector, called the zoopraxiscope, which showed short motion sequences on a screen using painted silhouettes corresponding to the attitudes of his photographs.

The most profound objections to Muybridge's analyses of movement, however, concerned their sequential representation. By presenting movement as a series of frozen attitudes he failed to allow for its fluid continuity in time and space. These objections were, to some extent, met by Muybridge's French contemporary Etienne-Jules Marey who, in 1882, published the first of his 'chronophotographs' in *La Nature* – the journal that had published Muybridge's galloping horse photographs four years earlier.[42] Marey's innovation was to combine the different phases of a movement on a single immobile plate, so that each phase was shown in the correct spatial relation to those that preceded and followed it (fig. 33). Marey's technique represented the entire trajectory of a movement and allowed it to be

Fig. 33 Etienne-Jules Marey, *Jump*, 1890–91, chronophotograph, negative 12 × 9 cm, Paris, Collège de France

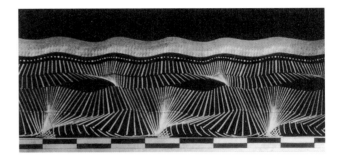

Fig. 34 Etienne-Jules Marey, *Joinville Soldier Walking*, 1883, chronophotograph, negative 13 × 18 cm, Paris, Collège de France

measured and analysed. In some of his most arresting and beautiful images he reduced his models to graphic notation by dressing them in black and by drawing white lines down their limbs (fig. 34). Marey's methods and aims were considerably more scientific than Muybridge's. His experiments were backed by the French military, who provided many of his models, and the analysis of his data resulted in the reform of training methods as well as mechanical explanations for such phenomena as our tendency to break into a run rather than walk at too fast a pace. But Marey's chronophotographs had repercussions well beyond the training manuals of the French army, for they seemed to provide an entirely new way of presenting motion and of visualising the passage of time.

Marey's images had their most powerful influence on artists after his death in the early years of the twentieth century, but their echoes can also be seen in

Cat. no. 23 Edgar Degas (1834–1917), *Ballet Dancers*
Probably 1890–1900, oil on canvas, 72.4 × 73 cm
London, National Gallery

a number of works produced by Degas in the last decade of the nineteenth.[43] Degas took photographs himself, making use of the medium in a variety of ways. He was certainly aware of Muybridge's experiments: he made two drawings of horses from photographs in *Animal Locomotion* and used others for sculptures.[44] Throughout his career, as attested by his recurrent concentration on dancers and horses, he addressed the problem of representing motion. 'My chief interest in dancers', he is reported to have told his dealer Vollard, 'lies in rendering movement and painting pretty clothes'.[45] Given these preoccupations, it would not be surprising if Degas had been aware of Marey's work; images such as *Three Dancers* (fig. 35) certainly suggest the influence of chronophotography in the overlapping forms of the near-identical dancers.

who seem to describe a single twisting movement. A similar effect is created in his late, unfinished *Ballet Dancers* (cat. no. 23) which, enhanced by the repeated shock of red hair, suggests the progress of a single dancer from background to foreground.[46] But although Degas may have been responding to Marey's photographs, there is no firm evidence that he knew them and it seems just as likely that he achieved these effects independently. The works reflect the fact they were made in the studio. Away from the subjects actually represented, Degas was repeating, reversing and tracing old figure studies, possibly taken from the same model, or drawing from sculptures, including different views of the same figure within the same image. His aims certainly included the representation and evocation of movement, and he achieved this through the rhythms of repetition and progression, but not in any way that must presuppose the influence of chronophotography.

If the link between Degas's late works and chronophotography is perhaps more apparent than real, the same can not be said for its influence on the work of the Italian Futurists. In the first of their numerous manifestos, published in 1910, they proclaimed that their subject would no longer be 'a fixed moment in universal dynamism. It shall simply be the *dynamic sensation itself* .... Indeed all things move, all things run, all things are rapidly changing. A profile is never motionless before our eyes, but constantly appears and disappears ... a running horse has not four legs but twenty and their movements are triangular.'[47] The Futurists sought a means of representation that denied the 'fixed moment' and that 'totally [did] away with the unities of time and place'.[48] This was not the first artistic movement of the twentieth century to challenge the spatial and temporal conventions of painting as the Futurists depended on their Cubist antecedents for many of their ideas and for their visual realisation. But unlike the Cubists, the Futurists' principal preoccupation was motion. In the words of Gino Severini, writing in 1913:

> One of our most systematic Futurist characteristics ... is that of expressing *sensations of movement*. Indeed one of the effects of science, which has transformed our sensibility and which has led to the majority of our Futurist truths is *speed*.[49]

The visual language used by the Futurists to convey these 'sensations of movement' had various sources, but chief among them was the iconography of movement and passing time established by Marey's chronophotographs. This is most clearly seen in certain paintings by Giacoma Balla such as *Dynamism of a Dog on a Leash* (fig. 36), whose subject seems curiously homely when measured against the Futurists' rhetorical glorification of technology and mechanisation. In the same way, despite Severini's appeal to science and speed, the motif that he explored most persistently in these years was the dance.

In his *Dynamism of a Dancer*, painted in Paris (cat. no. 24, overleaf), Severini uses multifaceted forms slicing into each other, which, while clearly deriving from Cubism, are here used to suggest the staccato rhythms of a high-kicking dance.[50] The dancer's yellow-

Fig. 35 Edgar Degas, *Three Dancers*, c.1888–93, pastel on paper, 47 × 30.8 cm, Tampa, Collection of Catherine and David. A. Straz Jr

Cat. no. 24 Gino Severini (1883–1966). *Dynamism of a Dancer*
1912. oil on canvas. 60 × 45 cm
Milan. Civico Museo d'Arte Contemporanea. Collezione Jucker

stockinged legs, high-heeled shoes and outstretched arms are all repeated to denote their jerky movement.

The Futurists' concerns were inspired by scientific, technological and cultural developments – from the telegraph and automobile to the theoretical challenges to Newtonian physics – that were creating new modes of thinking about time and space. Although their visual language appeared dependent on photographic discoveries, superimposing stages of a movement by artists was not new. In Ruben's sheet of dancers (cat. no. 21) the legs of some of the spinning couples have multiplied themselves in a manner entirely analogous to those of Severini's dancer, and Rubens was certainly not alone.

When sketching or drawing moving figures, artists have frequently resorted to depicting arms or legs in more than one position apparently simultaneously. As a means of notating movement – if not its representation in a finished work of art – the sequential overlapping of limbs or shapes has a long history. A fascinating manuscript of the late sixteenth century, based on Leonardo's writings, contains a series of drawings illustrating his theories of human movement that is precisely equivalent to Marey's chronophotographs (fig. 37).[51] There is even an attempt to illustrate the trajectories of the depicted movements in graphic form with a system of arcs and lines. In the National Gallery there is also a fascinating example of a finished painting which seems to use

Fig. 37 After Leonardo. *Huygens MS folio 22*. 1560–80. brown ink over black chalk on paper. 13.4 × 18.3 cm. New York. The Pierpoint Morgan Library

Fig. 38 Fra Filippo Lippi. *The Annunciation* (detail). late 1450s?, tempera on wood. 68.5 × 152 cm. London. National Gallery

superimposed stages of a movement, challenging the notion that this means of visualisation was unavailable before the age of the camera. In Filippo Lippi's *Annunciation* (fig. 38), painted in the mid-fifteenth century, the artist has represented the moment of the Virgin's conception. The dove of the Holy Spirit is shown descending from heaven in a gilded circle about to be received by a small radiating hole in Mary's dress. But it is how Lippi has described the descent that is most interesting in the present context: he shows the dove's trajectory through a series of overlapping circles describing, its journey through space and time in a way that anticipates the visual language of the Futurists by 450 years.

Fig. 36 Giacoma Balla. *Dynamism of a Dog on a Leash*. 1912. oil on canvas. 90.8 × 110.2 cm. Buffalo. Albright Knox Art Gallery

Time to Look

WHEN, AT THE END OF THE FIFTEENTH CENTURY, Leonardo da Vinci considered the relative merits of painting and poetry, he argued that one of the principal points in painting's favour was its ability to communicate in an instant: 'The poet in describing the beauty and ugliness of any figure can only show it to you consecutively, bit by bit, while the painter can display it all at once.'[1]

The notion that a painting can be taken in 'at a glance' has been much repeated. The Florentine Benedetto Varchi, when debating the respective merits of painting and sculpture in 1547, recommended the ability of painting to present multiple dimensions to the viewer in a single glance. In the seventeenth century Poussin, writing about the envisaged decoration of the Grand Galerie at the Louvre, noted approvingly that the width of the gallery would not prevent spectators seeing the ceiling picture in a glance – *un coup d'oeil*.[2] When, in the eighteenth century, writers such as Lessing came to distinguish systematically between the 'arts of time', such as music and poetry, and painting – an 'art of space' – it was the manner in which the respective arts communicated their meaning over time that was seen as their defining characteristic: music and poetry unfolding over time; paintings presenting themselves in an instant.

But despite the generally held belief that we see things instantaneously, this is not the case. We vastly overestimate the amount of information we take in 'at a glance' – even one lasting some seconds. According to one study, 'What we actually see is a very rough picture with a few spots in clear detail. What we feel we see is a large picture which is everywhere as clear in detail as the favourite spot on which we concentrate our attention.'[3]

HOW WE SEE

Looking is a process that takes time, and the nature of the process is conditioned by the way we see.[4] Humans only see things clearly in the centre of their visual field and within a surprisingly narrow band. Visual acuity is best for objects within a visual angle of one or two degrees (called foveal vision – the nail of a finger held at arm's length is approximately one degree across), and drops off dramatically away from the centre. Fix your eyes on the word HERE and you will notice that those around it become less clear the further they are away. In practice this means that if you are standing two metres away from a painting, at any one time you will only be seeing an approximately circular area of about five centimetres across with optimum sharpness. When we look at a painting – or anything else – we scan it, moving our eyes across the surface to build up a mental picture of the whole. For those areas we do not direct our eyes towards, we have to rely on the cruder representation provided by non-foveal vision. This scanning is not a smooth sweep like a panning camera, but is conducted in a series of jumps, known as saccades. Saccades happen very quickly: a ten-degree saccade takes about 45 milliseconds. In looking at a picture the eyes pause (or fixate), jump, then pause again, and it is only during these fixations that visual information is taken in and

Fig. 39 Paul Delaroche, *The Execution of Lady Jane Grey*, 1833, oil on canvas, 246 × 297 cm, London, National Gallery

BELOW LEFT Diagram showing the fixations of seventeen subjects looking at Delaroche's *The Execution of Lady Jane Grey* for 12 seconds. There is a characteristic clustering of fixations on the faces of the figures, but almost equal regard has been paid to the area – essential to the painting's meaning – of the executioner's block.
BELOW RIGHT Fixations and scan-paths of three participants looking at the painting for 6 seconds. The path of the eye appears to be directed by the painting's composition, apparently following the gaze of the executioner, and by meaning: moving between the executioner's block and axe. Most noticeable are the eye movements between the block and Lady Jane's head.

processed. The length of each fixation is normally a fraction of a second, but this can vary considerably. According to the existing data, the average fixation when looking at complex pictures, such as paintings, lasts about 300 milliseconds.

Although the accurate measurement of eye movements has only been possible in the last few decades, this process of vision has been recognised for centuries. Here is Pietro Cataneo writing in a treatise on perspective published in Venice in 1567:

> Note that in whatever thing one looks at one cannot see all its parts at a glance but one judges with the eye one part at a time so that seeing the head of a man one cannot judge the mouth, the eyes, the nose and its other parts at a glance but if one wishes to judge the nose one will fix the

eye on that and similarly wishing to judge the mouth one will fix the eye on that and thus it will be necessary to repeat the process for all the parts one by one.[5]

The source of this accurate description of the process of looking was derived from the work of the Islamic scholar of optics known in the West as Alhazen (956–1039) whose work was available in Latin from the twelfth century. Alhazen, and those that followed him, divided the process of vision into two parts: the first glance (*aspectus*), which provides a general idea of the field of view, and scrutiny (*inuitio obtutus*), defined as a series of individual observations leading to clear visual perception. Psychologists today maintain this distinction between the initial global – and crude –

perception of an image using the information gathered in the first fixation, and the fleshing out of objects of interest in subsequent fixations. The way the eyes move over an image also seems to change over time. In the early stages of looking, the eyes jump further and pause more briefly as they engage in what has been described as a diversive exploration. As the viewing proceeds, fixations tend to become longer and more concentrated as particular areas are explored.

HOLDING THE GAZE AND DIRECTING THE EYE

Alhazen's division of the process of viewing into 'the glance' and 'scrutiny' explains how, although the idea that paintings could be grasped 'in an instant' persisted, it was also recognised that looking took time. The seventeenth-century French theorist Roger de Piles used the same theory to describe the way a painting should act on the beholder. For him a painting should attract viewers from the first glance (on which he placed great emphasis), but it also needed to keep them standing in front of it.

Over two hundred years earlier, in the first treatise on painting of the Renaissance, the Florentine Alberti stated that one of painting's principal aims should be to 'hold the eye of the learned and unlearned spectator for a long while with a certain sense of pleasure and emotion'. One way to achieve this was to include a wealth of detail: 'when the spectators dwell on observing all the details, then the painter's richness will acquire favour.' But Alberti also suggested ways an artist could not only hold the gaze of the spectator but also direct it:

> Then I like there to be someone in the 'historia' who tells the spectators what is going on, and either beckons them with his hand to look … or points to some danger or remarkable thing in the picture, or by gestures invites you to laugh or weep with them.[6]

The idea that an artist can direct the eye of the spectator has become a commonplace of art criticism, and Alberti's pointing figures are only the most blatant of the devices artists have used to achieve this end. Paths and rivers in landscapes 'lead the eye' back into the distance; tonal contrasts and compositional lines are described as performing similar functions. In the eighteenth century, French Classicist critics such as Dandré-Bardon discussed a wide range of formal devices, from composition to colour, entirely in terms of controlling the spectator's eye:

> The grouping of figures should aim to give the composition a pyramidal form … one of the principal aims of the linking of the figure groups is to lead the eye of the spectator to the hero of the subject – an operation that is well performed by a diagonal leading into the picture.[7]

This way of considering a painting's composition achieved perhaps its most extreme formulation in the writings of the critic Diderot in the 1760s. For Diderot every composition has a 'line of liaison' which, he almost seemed to claim, is the path along

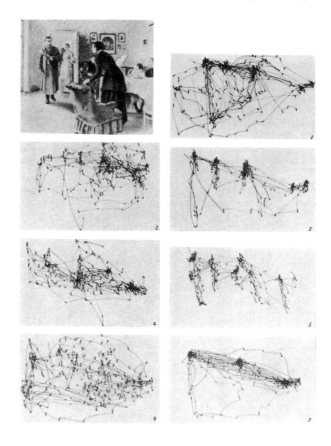

Fig. 40 From Alfred Yarbus, *Eye Movements and Vision*, 1965. The diagrams show the eye movements over three minutes of the same viewer (1) during a free viewing of Repin's *The Unexpected Visitor* and after being asked to: (2) estimate the material circumstances of the characters; (3) guess their ages; (4) surmise what the family had been doing before the 'visitor's' arrival; (5) remember the clothes; (6) remember the position of the people and objects; and (7) estimate how long the 'visitor' had been away.

Fig. 41 Aelburt Cuyp, *The Maas at Dordrecht in a Storm,*
*c.*1645–50, oil on oak, 49.8 × 74.4 cm, London, National Gallery

BELOW LEFT Fixations of three viewers looking at Cuyp's painting for
6 seconds. The radius of the circles relates to the duration of each
fixation (the larger the circle the longer the fixation), varying from
100 milliseconds to 1 second for the atypically large white circle. No
two people will ever see a painting in the same way. The viewer
represented in white concentrated on the right side of the painting
with its view of Dordrecht, barely looking to the left.
BELOW RIGHT Data from fifteen subjects looking at the same
painting, with areas of fixation illuminated. The sky, with the
exception of the lightning flash, was virtually ignored. Hardly any
of the viewers can have seen the pair of flying birds.

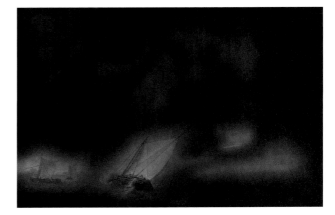

which the spectators' eyes will be directed, whether
they like it or not.

> If this line [of liaison] ... bends, folds over onto
> itself, twists, is agitated, if its circumvolutions
> are diminutive, multiple, rectilinear and
> angular, the composition will be ambiguous and
> obscure; the eye wandering at random through a
> labyrinth, bewildered, will find it difficult to
> grasp the connections .... A well-ordered
> composition will always have but one true line of
> liaison: and it will serve as a guide to anyone
> looking at it as well as to anyone attempting to
> describe it.[8]

What evidence there is suggests that such ideas bear
little relation to the way our eyes actually travel
over paintings. This does not mean that they need
be entirely spurious, but that they are mental
reconstructions made retroactively during the
process of looking. A leading diagonal – and its
compositional intention – can be recognised without
the eye being forced to travel along it.

EYE MOVEMENTS

Exploring whether a painting can influence the way
our eyes move over it – and the other factors that
determine scan-paths and fixations – is one of the
aims of the experiment conducted by the Applied
Vision Research Unit from the Institute of Behavioural
Sciences, Derby, during the period of this exhibition.
The use of an eye-tracking machine and computer
software allows members of the public to explore
their own eye movements as they look at pictures in
the largest eye-tracking experiment ever conducted.
It would be foolish to attempt to anticipate the
experiment's results, but previous studies have
already reached some tentative conclusions about the
way we look at pictures.

The path that our eyes take over a picture's
surface is not random – if it were it would not be
particularly interesting. When looking at a picture
we fixate upon one area, move our eyes and then
fixate upon another, but we do not scan the picture
evenly, centimetre by centimetre: instead our eyes

seek out and concentrate on particular areas. The mechanism with which, during each fixation, we select the next area to be fixated upon, is not fully understood, but it is a process controlled (consciously or unconsciously) by ourselves. We fixate on those areas that contain most 'information', often completely ignoring areas we judge unimportant. In paintings that include figures, fixations will usually be concentrated on their faces, and within faces they will usually cluster around the eyes and mouth (fig. 39). Exactly which areas of a painting attract most fixations will depend on what information is being sought. In a famous experiment conducted in the 1960s, the Russian Alfred Yarbus recorded a subject's eye movements as he looked at a painting called *The Unexpected Visitor* by Ilya Repin. Yarbus gave a number of prompts to the viewer, asking him, for example, to judge the material circumstances of the family in the painting, to estimate their ages, and to remember the position of the people and objects in the room. In each case the pattern of eye movements altered dramatically (fig. 40).

The fact that our eye movements are governed by intention has a number of important repercussions. Because we are all different and have different expectations, knowledge and interests when we come to a painting (fig. 41), no two people will actually see the same image. Someone looking at a painting to explore an artist's technique will see something different from the person trying to ascertain its subject matter. When connoisseurs are described as having a 'good eye' – meaning that they are able to attribute works to particular artists – it does not mean that their eyes work better than anyone else's, indeed they can be hopelessly myopic. The brain of someone with a 'good eye' has been trained to recognise – and find 'interesting' – the characteristic stylistic tics and habits of a wide range of painters, and so one might suppose that it is to these areas of particular interest that their eyes will move. Those less expert would be less likely to find such areas informative or interesting.

It is not only intention that governs the path viewer's eyes take; there are other contributing factors. There is some evidence, for example, to suggest that our brains order our fixations in such a way as to minimise the total scan pathway, so that we can collect the maximum amount of visual information with the minimum amount of eye movement.[9] Obviously, the painting being looked at also influences the way that eyes travel over it, even if not in the manner envisaged by Diderot. For example, experiments have suggested that the length of fixations varies depending on the type of picture being looked at: complex cluttered images lead to shorter fixations than simpler ones.[10]

However fascinating the analyses of how we look at pictures produced by eye-tracking experiments, they can only present a partial explanation of the process. Measuring eye movements usually requires the subject to stay still and, for obvious reasons, subjects are usually observed as they scan reproductions of paintings. If you observe people looking at pictures in a gallery, however, they are often on the move: stepping up to get a closer look or standing back to see the fuller picture. When looking at a representational painting we are also looking at two separate things: what is represented in the painting and the paint itself – the marks of the brush on the panel or canvas. Psychologists of vision tell us that it is impossible to perceive both simultaneously as we either perceive objects in space or a flat pattern of different colours and brushstrokes, but clearly one of the pleasures of looking at paintings is the way they encourage us to switch from one way of looking to another. But this is a switch that would be difficult, if not impossible, for any eye-tracking device to recognise.

THEY ARE PERFECTLY SAFE   THIS IS A STILL

Art of Time?

THE FACT THAT LOOKING TAKES TIME suggests a possible solution to the problem of how painters can put time in their paintings. When depicting both stories and movement it could be argued that artists exploit the time it takes to view a painting. Returning to earlier examples, when Giovanni di Paolo paints Saint John the Baptist twice in the same painting, it is tempting to imagine that the viewer provides the lapse in narrative time in the act of looking from one figure to the next. When we talk of Poussin 'extending the moment' in his painting of the *Gathering of the Manna*, it is easy to consider that this extension is linked to the temporal process of looking from one group of figures to the next. Furthermore, the idea that when looking at the steps of a movement in sequence, the viewer can act like a film projector – putting the figures into motion as the eye moves from one to the next – also equates time that the viewer spends in front of the picture with the imaginary time within the painting. Following these observations you might even argue that because seeing is not instantaneous, but a process that takes time in which different parts of the image are viewed in succession, painting, like music and poetry, could be described as an 'art of time'. But any such argument leads to confusion.

Any attempt to link the time we look at a painting with the narrative time within it results in absurdities. The time it takes to move our eyes from the figure of Saint John at the city gate to the figure of him in the mountains bears no relation to the time it would have taken him to get there. Or to take a contrary example, no one would suggest that we should only look at Rembrandt's *Belshazzar's Feast* (cat. no. 10) for the split second it is clearly intended to represent. Determining the amount of time in a painting is dependent upon us interpreting the event represented. This is a reconstruction based on the process of looking: not one determined by it. We can 'read' Giovanni di Paolo's (cat. no. 6) painting correctly whichever figure of Saint John we happen to fixate on first. We perceive the parts of a painting in succession but, crucially, the order of this succession is not determined (as it is when we listen to music) and it is essentially unimportant. A picture only makes sense because we understand – even if we cannot see clearly – that all its elements are co-existent.

We take time to look at paintings and we may read time into them, but we know that we are looking at stills where time has stopped and everyone is perfectly safe. A painting does after all exist, even if it cannot be seen, 'in an instant'. But paintings also exist over time, to be viewed again and again by generation after generation. Paintings as physical objects may be subject to time but what they show is not. It is this sense of time, frozen and preserved, that lies behind Hockney's *Picture Emphasising Stillness* (cat. no. 15). As the artist has observed, no matter how dramatic or dynamic a painting 'the figures are, and always will remain exactly where the painter put them'.

ENDNOTES

About Time

1. On the figure of Time see Saxl 1936, Panofsky 1939 and Lippincott 1999–2000, pp. 170–181.
2. For the sundial and other instruments in Holbein's portrait see Foister et al. 1997, pp 33–5. Amberger's portrait of Matthäus Schwarz the Elder, 1542 (Madrid, Thyssen-Bornemisza Collection) records the sitter's age as 45 years, 30 days and 21¾ hours.
3. Among the most sophisticated examples are the *trompe l'oeil* still lifes by the Dutch specialist Cornelis Gijsbrechts in which canvases showing *vanitas* still lifes are painted as if peeling from their stretchers. See Koester 2000, pp. 31–7.

Story Time

1. On the *Royal Standard of Ur* see Perkins 1957. On early narrative in the Near East see Winter 1985.
2. Kauffmann 1975, no. 66. Gibson et al. 1992. The three other sheets from the series are in New York (Pierpoint Morgan Library, M 521 and M 724) and London (British Library ADD. MS 37472(1)). On early Biblical illustration see Lowden 1999.
3. See Henderson 1992.
4. On the varied arrangement of narrative cycles in churches and chapels see Lavin 1990.
5. Spencer-Longhurst 1993, p. 53.
6. See Burke 1955, p. 216 and Kunzle 1973.
7. Goodison 1997, pp. 114–5. Paulson 1991, pp. 218–9.
8. Treble 1978, cat. no. 10.
9. See Ruskin 1858, p. 26. In his review of the Royal Academy exhibition of 1858, his discussion of Egg's paintings immediately precedes his review of Anna Blunden's *Past and Present*.
10. Ibid.
11. *Athenaeum*, 1 May 1858, p. 566.
12. Davies 1961, pp. 243–5. Dunkerton et al. 1991, pp. 278–80.
13. The terminology used to describe the types of pictorial narration can be confusing. Different writers have used different terms to describe the same narrative techniques and, more confusingly, used the same terms to describe different techniques. The attempts to arrive at precise definitions have been mostly in relation to ancient and early Christian art. For examples see Wickhoff 1900 and Weitzmann 1970, in which each offer a threefold division of narrative art, but use different terms for their categories. Two useful summaries of current terminology are provided in Andrews 1995, pp. 120–6, and Stansbury-O'Donnell 1999, pp. 1–7.
14. See James Barry's fourth lecture to the Royal Academy, Barry 1809, p. 454. Michelangelo combined the scenes of the Fall of Man and the Expulsion from Paradise against a single landscape on the Sistine Chapel ceiling. Raphael shows Saint Peter and the Angel twice in his *Liberation of Saint Peter* in the *Stanza Eliodoro*, also in the Vatican.
15. On the extensive use of continuous narrative in the fifteenth century, see Andrews 1995.
16. Quoted in McMahon 1956 (Cod. Urb. 47v). Cited and translated in Gombrich 1999, p. 17. Although no fresco survives in which Leonardo follows his own advice, it is closely adhered to by his pupil Bernardino Luini in his fresco of *Golgotha* in Sta Maria degli Angioli in Lugano.
17. Maclaren/Brown 1991, pp. 502–3. Spicer/Orr 1997, cat. no. 50.
18. Junius 1991, vol. 1, p. 275.
19. This image is discussed by Robert 1881, p. 16 and by Weitzmann 1970, note 7, p. 13.
20. Davies 1961, pp. 532–3: Dunkerton et al. 1991, pp. 164.
21. On the relation between the theories of poetry and painting see Lee 1967, Puttfarken 1981 and Puttfarken 1985, esp. pp 1–37.
22. Bellori 1732, pp. 120ff. Discussed in Dowley 1976, esp. pp. 320–3.
23. Poussin letter to Fréart de Chantelou, 1639, in *Correspondance de Nicolas Poussin* ed. C. Jouanny, Paris, 1911, quoted in Blunt 1958, p. 223.
24. Félibien 1669, pp. 424–25, quoted in Puttfarken 1985, pp. 8–9. On Poussin's painting in relation to time see also Dowley 1997.
25. 'A notion of the Historical Draught, or Tabulature of the Judgement of Hercules' in Shaftesbury 1714. The painting in the exhibition is a copy also made by Matteis for Shaftesbury, completed on 29 June 1712 – three months after he had delivered the original (now in the Ashmolean Museum, Oxford). The copy had been planned as a gift for Shaftesbury's patron Lord Somers, but was actually sold for 120 ducats (£24) to his friend Sir John Cropley. See Wind 1938, O'Connell 1988 and Pestelli 1990.
26. Lessing 1984, esp. pp. 19–22.
27. Brown et al. 1991, cat. no. 22. On the use by Rembrandt and his pupils of moments of reversal or *peripatea* see Blankert 1982, pp. 34–6.
28. Baker/Henry 1995, p. 95. Mancini *Considerazioni sulla pittura*, trs. in Hibbard 1983, p. 350, describes the work as being produced for the market (*per vendere*). On the various interpretations of the picture see Spear 1985, pp. 22–7.
29. Giovanni Baglione, 1642, trs. in Hibbard 1983, p. 352.

Moment and Movement

1. For the high-speed photography of Harold Edgerton (1903–90) see Jussim/Kayafas 1987.
2. Letter from Etienne-Jules Marey to Gaston Tissandier, editor of *La Nature*, 18 December 1878 – four days after the first of Muybridge's photographs of galloping horses were published. Quoted in Braun 1992, p. 47.
3. O.W. Holmes 'The Human Wheel, its spokes and felloes' in *Atlantic Monthly*, vol. 11 (May 1863), quoted in Newhall 1944, p. 41.
4. G.A. Sala in the *New York Tribune*, reprinted in the *San Francisco Bulletin*, 24 June 1882. Quoted in Mozley 1979, pp. xxiii–xxiv.
5. See Hungerford 1999, pp. 202–8.
6. From Rodin's conversations with Paul Gsell quoted in Scharf 1968, pp. 173–4.
7. Giulio Mancini *Considerazioni sulla pittura* MS of c.1617–21, trs. in Hibbard 1983, p. 350.
8. Mahon 1951, p. 229.
9. Richter 1939, no. 369, p 264.
10. Fehl 1992, p. 69.
11. Merriman 1980, cat. nos. 303–22.
12. Lowenthal 1983, McGee 1991. On Cornelis's preoccupations at the time see Van Mander 1994, pp. 428–30.
13. Finaldi/Kitson 1997, cat. no. 52.
14. Melia/Luckhardt 1994, no. 10, Livingstone 1996, pp. 44–6.
15. Eugène Veron *L'esthetique*, Paris,

1878, quoted in Braun 1992, p. 272.

16. W. de W. Abney 'Are instantaneous photographs true?' in *International Annual of Anthony's Photographic Bulletin* vol. 2 (1889), pp. 285–7, quoted in Newhall 1944.

17. MacCurdy 1938, pp. 230–1.

18. Leonardo *Codice Atlantico* fol. 1002 trs. in Andrews 1995, p. 152, note 13.

19. Quoted in Kemp 1989, p. 67.

20. Ibid.

21. For example in Gombrich 1977, pp. 191–2. For a discussion of blurred wheel spokes in Velázquez's and other seventeenth-century paintings see: Bedaux 1992 and Takahashi 1982.

22. Philips Angel, *Lof der schilder-konst*, Leiden 1642. The relevant passage is quoted in Bedaux 1992, p. 301.

23. The quotation cited by Bedaux 1992, note 8, p. 301 comes from Karel van Mander's adaptation of Pliny, *Het leren der oude antijcke doorluchtighe schilders*, 1603, the version most likely to have been known by Angel.

24. Krempel 2000, cat. no. D.2.

25. Hoogstraten 1678, p. 163 quoted in Bedaux 1992, p. 301.

26. Hall 2000, cat. no. 25

27. Egerton 1998, pp. 316–25. As it happens Turner saw Stubbs's painting when he visited Saltram in 1813 during a tour of Devon with his friend Cyrus Redding. Redding records that Turner passed the 'best paintings' in silence but paused in front of Stubbs's *Phaeton* to make the monosyllabic judgement 'fine' (Hall 2000, p. 122).

28. Written under the pen-name Michael Angelo Titmarsh, 'May Gambols; or, Titmarsh in the Picture Galleries', *Fraser's Magazine*, June 1844, pp. 712–3.

29. *Morning Chronicle* quoted in Butler/Joll 1984.

30. Eastlake to Wornum, 15 June 1857 (National Gallery Archive), quoted in Gage 1972, p. 66.

31. G.D. Leslie, *The Inner Life of the Royal Academy*, 1914, pp. 144–5.

32. The anecdote was told by Mrs John Simon to both George Richmond and John Ruskin, see Egerton 1998, pp. 318–19.

33. Scharf 1968, pp. 127–33.

34. *Paris-Journal*, 7 May 1874, quoted in Scharf 1968, p. 129.

35. Bowron 1990, p. 122. Rapetti/Eggum 1991, pp. 103–4. For Munch's use of photography see Eggum 1989, although this does not consider Munch's response to the photographic blur.

36. Quoted in Rapetti 1991, p. 102.

37. Verdi 1995, cat. no. 28.

38. Ibid.

39. John Ruskin, *Notes on the Louvre*, 1849 in Cook/Wedderburn 1903–12, p. 470–1.

40. Held 1986, cat. nos. 193–4.

41. Mozley 1979. For a discussion of the scientific credentials of Muybridge's *Animal Locomotion* see Braun 1992, pp. 228–62.

42. See Braun 1992.

43. Ibid, p. 272, note 2 and Kendall 1996, p. 188.

44. For Degas and Muybridge see Scharf 1968, pp. 158–60.

45. Vollard 1937, p. 87.

46. Kendall 1996, cat. no. 84. See also chapter 3 and pp. 186–8 on Degas's late technique and practice.

47. Umberto Boccioni, Carlo Carra, Luigi Russolo, Giacomo Balla and Gino Severini, *La pittura futurista: Manifesto tecnico*, Milan, 11 April 1910, trs. in Apollonio 1973, pp. 27–8.

48. Gino Severini, *Le analogie plastiche del dinamismo*, 1914, trs. in Apollonio 1973, p. 121.

49. Apollonio 1973, p. 124.

50. Fonti 1988, cat. no. 106

51. See Panofsky 1940.

Time to Look

1. Quoted in Richter 1939, no. 35, p. 79.

2. Letter to Sublet de Noyers c.1642, in Félibien 1725, pp. 279ff, trs. in Merot 1990, pp. 310–1.

3. Henry Quastler 'Studies of Human Channel Capacity', n.d., quoted in Gombrich 1982, p. 50.

4. Available introductions to the science of vision and perception include: Gregory 1997 and Roth/Bruce 1995. A useful guide to the early sources is Wade 1998. See also Solso 1996 for an excellent introduction to perception and the visual arts, esp. chapter 6 on eye movements, from which the statistics that follow are taken.

5. Pietro Cataneo *L'architettura*, Venice 1567, quoted in Fragenberg 1986, p. 151.

6. Alberti 1991, pp. 75–8.

7. Dandré-Bardon 1765, pp. 107–8.

8. Goodman 1995, p. 152.

9. Stark/Ellis 1981, cited in Solso, 1996, p. 143.

10. F. Molnar in *Perception visuelle de l'unité*, Thesis University of Nanterre, 1974, calculated that the mean duration of eye fixations looking at 'Baroque' paintings was 60 milliseconds briefer than when looking at 'Classical' images. Cited in Solso 1996, pp. 154–5 and fig. 6.14.

BIBLIOGRAPHY

Alberti 1991 Alberti. *On Painting*. trs. C. Grayson. ed. Martin Kemp. London. 1991

Andrews 1995 Lew Andrews. *Story and Space in Renaissance Art: The Rebirth of Continuous Narrative*. Cambridge. 1995

Apollonio 1973 *Futurist Manifestos*. ed. Umbro Apollonio. London. 1973

Baker/Henry 1995 Christopher Baker and Tom Henry. *The National Gallery Complete Illustrated Catalogue*. London. 1995

Barry 1809 James Barry. *Works of James Barry Esq*. London. 1809

Bedaux 1992 Jean-Baptiste Bedaux 'Velázquez's *Fable of Arachne* (*Las Hilanderas*): a continuing story' in *Simiolus*. vol. 21. no. 4 (1992). pp. 296–305

Bellori 1732 Giovanni Pietro Bellori. *Dafne transformata in Lauro* published with his *Vita di Carlo Maratti Pittore*. Rome. 1732

Blankert 1982 Albert Blankert. *Ferdinand Bol (1616–1680): Rembrandt's Pupil*. trs. Ina Rike. Doornspijk. 1982

Blunt 1958 A. Blunt. *Nicolas Poussin*. London and New York. 1958

Bowron 1990 Edgar Peters Bowron. *European Paintings before 1900 in the Fogg Art Museum*. Cambridge. Mass.. 1990

Braun 1992 Marta Braun. *Picturing Time: the work of Etienne-Jules Marey (1830–1904)*. Chicago and London. 1992

Brown et al. 1991 *Rembrandt: The Master and his Workshop: Paintings*. exh. cat.. ed. C. Brown. J. Kelch and P. Van Thiel. New Haven and London. 1991

Burke 1955 *William Hogarth: The Analysis of Beauty ... and Autobiographical Notes*. ed. Joseph Burke. Oxford. 1955

Butler/Joll 1984 Martin Butler and Evelyn Joll. *The Paintings of J.M.W. Turner*. New Haven and London. 1984

Cook/Wedderburn 1903–12 *The Works of John Ruskin*. vol. XII of XXXIX. ed.. E.T. Cook and A. Wedderburn. London. 1903–12

Dandré-Bardon 1765 Dandré-Bardon. *Traité de Peinture, suivi d'un essai sur la sculpture*. Paris. 1765

Davies 1961 Martin Davies. *National Gallery Catalogues: The Earlier Italian Schools*. London. 1961

Dowley 1976 Francis H. Dowley 'The Moment in Eighteenth-Century Art Criticism' in *Studies in Eighteenth-Century Culture*. vol. 5 (1976). pp. 317–36

Dowley 1997 Francis H. Dowley 'Thoughts on Poussin, time and narrative' in *Simiolus*. vol. 25. no. 4 (1997). pp. 329–48

Dunkerton et al. 1991 Jill Dunkerton. Susan Foister. Dillian Gordon and Nicholas Penny. *Giotto to Dürer, Early Renaissance Painting in The National Gallery*. London. 1991

Egerton 1998 Judy Egerton. *National Gallery Catalogues: The British School*. London. 1998

Eggum 1989 Arne Eggum. *Munch and Photography*. trs. Birgit Holm. New Haven and London. 1989

Fehl 1992 Phillip Fehl 'The Bacchanals of Alfonso I D'Este' in *Decorum and Wit: The Poetry of Venetian Painting*. Vienna. 1992. pp. 46–87

Félibien 1669 Félibien. *Conférences de l'Academie Royale de Peinture et de Sculpture*. vol. V. Paris. 1669

Félibien 1725 Félibien. *Entretiens sur les Vies ... des plus excellens Peintres....* vol. IV. Trevaux. 1725

Finaldi/Kitson 1997 *Discovering the Italian Baroque: The Denis Mahon Collection*. exh. cat.. eds. Gabriele Finaldi and Michael Kitson. National Gallery. London. 1997

Foister et al. 1997 *Holbein's Ambassadors*. exh. cat.. Susan Foister. Ashok Roy and Martin Wyld. National Gallery. London. 1998

Fonti 1988 Daniela Fonti. *Gino Severini: Catalogo ragionato*. cat. 106. Milan. 1988

Fragenberg 1986 Thomas Fragenberg 'The Image and the Moving Eye: Jean Pélerin (Viator) to Guidobaldo del Monte'. *JWCI* 49 (1986). pp. 150–171

Gage 1972 John Gage. *Turner: Rain, Steam and Speed*. London. 1972

Gibson et al. 1992 *The Eadwine Psalter: Text, Image and Monastic Culture in Twelfth-Century Canterbury*. eds. M. Gibson. T.A. Heslop and R.W. Pfaff. London and University Park 1992

Gombrich 1977 E.H. Gombrich. *Art and Illusion: a study in the psychology of pictorial representation*. London. 1977

Gombrich 1982 E.H. Gombrich 'Moment and Movement in Art' in *The Image and the Eye: Further studies in the psychology of pictorial representation*. Oxford. 1982

Gombrich 1999 E.H. Gombrich 'Paintings on Walls: Means and Ends in the History of Fresco Painting' in *The Uses of Images: Studies in the Social Function of Art and Visual Communication*. London. 1999. pp. 40–62

Goodison 1977 J.W. Goodison. *Fitzwilliam Museum Cambridge: Catalogue of Paintings*. vol. III. British School. Cambridge. 1977

Goodman 1995 *Diderot on Art vol II: The Salon of 1767*. trs. and ed. John Goodman. New Haven and London. 1995

Gregory 1997 Richard Gregory. *Eye and Brain: The Psychology of Seeing*. revised 5th edn.. Princeton. 1997

Hall 2000 *Fearful Symmetry: George Stubbs, painter of the English Enlightenment*. exh. cat.. ed. Nicholas H.J. Hall. New York. 2000

Held 1986 J. Held. *Rubens, Selected Drawings*. Oxford. 1986

Henderson 1992 George Henderson 'The textual basis of the picture leaves' in Gibson et al. 1992. pp. 35–42

Hibbard 1983 Howard Hibbard. *Caravaggio*. London. 1983

Hoogstraten 1678 Samuel van Hoogstraten. *Inleyding tot de hooge schoole der schilderkonst*. Rotterdam. 1678

Hungerford 1999 Constance Cain Hungerford, *Ernest Meissonier: Master in His Genre*. Cambridge. 1999

Junius 1991 Franciscus Junius, *The Literature of Classical Art*. eds. Keith Aldrich. Philip Fehl and Raina Fehl. Berkeley. 1991

Jussim/Kayafas 1987 Estelle Jussim and Guy Kayafas. *Stopping Time: The Photographs of Harold Edgerton*. New York. 1987

Kauffmann 1975 C.M. Kauffmann. *Romanesque Manuscripts. 1066–1190*. London. 1975

Kemp 1989 *Leonardo on Painting*. ed. Martin Kemp. New Haven and London. 1989

Kendall 1996 *Degas: Beyond Impressionism*. exh. cat.. Richard Kendall. National Gallery. London. 1996

Koester 2000 *Painted Illusions: The Art of Cornelis Gijsbrechts*. exh. cat.. O. Koester. National Gallery. London. 2000

Krempel 2000 Léon Krempel. *Nicolaes Maes*. Petersberg. 2000

Kunzle 1973 David Kunzle. *The Early Comic Strip: narrative strips and picture stories in the European broadsheet from c.1450 to 1825*. Berkeley. 1973

Lavin 1990 M.A. Lavin. *The Place of Narrative: mural decoration in Italian churches, 431–1600*. Chicago. 1990

Lee 1967 R.W. Lee. *Ut Pictura Poesis: The Humanistic Theory of Painting*. New York. 1967*Painting*. New York. 1967